Seeking Something Sacred

Managing Our Frustrations, Losses, And Fears

Joseph E. Talley

CSS Publishing Company, Inc., Lima, Ohio

Copyright © 2001 by
CSS Publishing Company, Inc.
Lima, Ohio

Library of Congress Cataloging-in-Publication Data

Talley, Joseph E.
    Seeking something sacred : managing our frustrations, losses, and fears / Joseph E. Talley.
        p.   cm.
    ISBN 0-7880-1874-4 (alk. paper)
    1. Pastoral psychology. I. Title.
BV4012 .T35   2001
248.8'6—dc21   2001037934
                                                                              CIP

For more information about CSS Publishing Company resources, visit our website at www.csspub.com.

ISBN 0-7880-1874-4   PRINTED IN U.S.A.

This writing is dedicated to
Daniel Absalon Talley
(January 23, 1986 — August 16, 1986)

The darkness and the light are both alike to Thee.
— Psalm 139:12 (KJV)

For God is light and in him is no darkness at all.
— 1 John 1:5 (KJV)

The Blacksmith

Is it you, oh God, who is the blacksmith of our souls
As you pound and pound again and again
While we lie on your immovable anvil?
Who but you could place us each
Carefully into the fire's hottest point,
Remember us and retrieve our remnants
To tremble once more under your mighty arm
As you hammer anew?

Dare we ask to be laid down from your hand
And set aside from your workbench
When you are the only smithy of souls?
I would call you terrible
But who, other than you, can see
What shape our souls must become?
Must you hammer and fire us
Until we no longer recognize our form
And only you recall our essence?

Must the banging and trembling go on
Until we see only the forger's mighty arm?
Or does it go on until we see not only
The forger's eye
But as the eye of the forger who sees us sees —
A sea of souls upon his mold?
Lord, perhaps you were once the potter and we the clay
But now, surely, you are the blacksmith of our souls.

(J.E.T.)

Acknowledgments

Acknowledgments and thanks go to Dr. Thomas E. McCollough, Professor Emeritus at Duke University, for urging me to do this writing; Dr. James B. Erb, Professor of Music Emeritus at the University of Richmond, for nurturance in the themes of thought in this book through choral music; and Dr. O. William Rhodenheiser, Professor of Religion Emeritus at the University of Richmond, who nurtured me in the relationship of psychology and religion. Thanks also go to Ms. Crystal S. Duchow who provided wonderful assistance in the final preparation of the manuscript.

Preface

This writing focuses on the absolute fragility of human life and, thus, the need to live this life grounded in that which is beyond it in order to contain the potential anxiety, despair, and rage resulting from the losses inherent in our human situation. I will address aspects of the causes and effects of human pain and suffering insofar as they may relate to God. This is neither a scholarly work nor a comprehensive reckoning with the topic. Ideas from other sources are credited in the manuscript and a References and Bibliography section is provided. My viewpoint is that of a theologically-oriented psychologist. Yet, I am writing also as one who, like most people, has experienced the fragility of human life firsthand.

A look at human pain and suffering in relation to God prompts an examination of what we usually might call "evil." Psychology has, I believe, something to offer concerning how we look at that which we call "bad" or "evil."

Might God work as a blacksmith with much less regard for our physical and psychological comfort than for that which is within us that is eternal? Perhaps human suffering works in the service of this soul and spirit though at the expense of our bodily or emotional pain. We don't like this possibility for many reasons. We expect for the most part that the reasons why something occurred are or will become understandable. With pain and suffering, ultimate reasons, if any exist, are often elusive. Consequently, we may conclude there can be no answers or even possible answers concerning "why." Pain that seems to have no meaning to it is more difficult to live with. Persons who suffer and cannot find some possible meanings for it suffer twice. They not only suffer, they also suffer about their suffering because there is no apparent purpose for it. They may become anxious, despairing, or enraged about their circumstances. Since all human beings will suffer in some way sooner or later, we are all candidates for anxiety, despair, and rage. I propose that we are more likely candidates for those feelings that are destructive of self or others when no theological context of meaning can be given to the felt loss. In its more developed form this theological context of meaning results in transformation of the self whereby identification with the God of self-sacrifice is at the core of the self and not self-interest alone.

Table Of Contents

Chapter 1

Our Situation In
The Human Condition

Human Life Is Very Fragile

In the very next moment life could change drastically and for-ever. Something seemingly horrible could and might happen in the very next moment. It has happened to me that way several times. Suddenly, with no advance warning, I had a hemorrhage causing initial total paralysis of the left side of my body and the permanent loss of the full functioning of my left arm and leg. Nothing could have been done to prevent it. Nothing could be done to completely restore the use of my body. Human life is very vulnerable.

One morning I looked at our infant son. He was six months and three weeks old and a very sturdy-looking, healthy boy show-ing no evidence of any problems. Within twelve hours he was dead. Dead, even though we had immediate access to a major medical center. The meningitis-like illness could not be seen nor were there any signs that he was ill. There was no warning. Everything was tried to save him. Nothing available could rescue him from the infection that consumed him. If he had been spared death, major brain damage was almost certain. Seemingly nothing could alter these circumstances. Nothing could be done to change it. He was dead. Human life is very fragile.

Once, with little prelude and completely unexpectedly, I felt an overwhelming sense of panic, dread, and terror. My heartbeat increased in speed and loudness until I thought I would have a heart attack. I couldn't sleep or eat. Ideas rushed through my mind and the physical sensations felt unbearable. Yet I could not escape them. I was terribly afraid. Suddenly my body felt beyond my own control. I, who had always felt supremely confident, felt vulner-able and frightened. I feared I was losing my sanity since I seemed to be no longer in control of my mind. Ideas popped in without the familiar sense that I was intending what came to mind to be there.

Many years later I understood that this was what today would be called a "panic attack." The life of the human mind has only limited control over itself. The sense of helplessness that this experience prompted and how I responded to it changed the way I looked at life, how I felt about life, and how I responded to experiencing the death of our son and the loss of parts of my physical functioning.

The experiential knowing that I could not control many things even within myself came to me clearly. Only reaching to that which is beyond human life seemed to allow me to live this human life with its fragility, vulnerability, and limited control. In all probability sooner or later some events like one of these will occur in your life or in the life of someone in your family. Although this thought causes discomfort, it will not help to avoid it and deny the realities that comprise human life and death.

Behind The Veil

Amidst the joys of day-to-day life and the sense of whatever we find pleasurable or good, there are also undeniable frustrations in this life and pains due to the losses we experience. Behind the veil of the drama of human life that is played out in the open, there is the inner life of anxieties and fears, desires and wishes. Much of this inner life is focused on specific or particular matters that would seem, if not petty, at least of minor importance to another. Yet some of these rumblings on the back burner of the mind have to do with the greatest of concerns. Philosophers, theologians, dramatists, as well as authors and artists of all types, have called our attention to these basic concerns for as long as we know of the existence of humanity.

Such concerns have been the focus of drawings on the walls of caves and rituals around primitive hunting expeditions, battles, and the planting and harvesting of crops. These concerns are in essence about survival. They are about life and death. Still, in modern life behind the facade of large cities with their immense buildings, advanced telecommunications, our routine travel in space, and the heretofore unimaginable computer technology, we are aware of these anxieties concerning life and death. They may not be in the forefront of our thoughts due to the myriad of distractions in carrying out the moment-to-moment "busyness" seemingly required of us, but somewhere in our minds we know these anxieties. Much of our mental and emotional energy is spent in the effort to ignore them, for they are unpleasant. They make us feel uncomfortable and therefore they disrupt our productivity. That is one of the last things the modern Western human being wants to happen.

If it is so unpleasant to look at such things, then why would we wish to bother to do so once again? To respond, it is because there is nothing more important to do than to re-examine that which is the most bothersome of concerns, if it might lead to being less uncomfortable about it. In short, we might feel better if we will first tolerate feeling worse while in the process of looking at what troubles us. We can master these anxieties better if we look them in the eye instead of trying to hide from them. Hiding from these troubles gives them more power over time. We become more and more convinced that we must never look at such anxieties, in part because we may have never looked at them carefully and reckoned with them and our possible options.

Looking at our anxieties does make it clear that there are some choices to be made. Perhaps we don't truly want these choices since the consequences of our decisions are so great. In fact, we *do* have these choices and we *do* make decisions. We can admit this, examine the options, and decide actively; or we can deny it, ignore conscious consideration of the possibilities, and decide passively by default. Then we must live with the consequences of deciding by way of not intentionally deciding.

Our fears will vary from person to person because they have a specific focus. Yet if we were to look at these fears in some detail and their histories in the context of our life experience, it is likely we would find that these fears relate in some way to the general anxieties experienced by all of humankind. Specific fears are often ways to manage more general anxieties about life and death by focusing the anxiety onto something particular. Perhaps then we feel the anxiety is more manageable because it's known in some way as a fear. We hope to exert at least some control over whatever is involved. When the anxiety is localized or focused and has become a specific fear of something, we then believe that it is more likely that we can do something to avoid whatever the possible horrible occurrence might be.

Thus much of our mental life, often outside our awareness, may be devoted to developing specific fears and focusing on how to manage them in order to avoid more unpleasant thoughts and feelings about something vague. We can't name it but we feel very helpless in the face of it in part *because* we cannot name it. Apparently we would rather have more immediate, particular fears than this vague something. In the face of it we feel helpless to a great extent because it is unknown. In all likelihood we have our fears in the conscious mind to keep the larger anxieties out of the conscious mind. So there is at least some "pay off" in a sense for having fears. They keep anxieties at arm's length and in the background of consciousness, if we are conscious of them at all. That we would do this is most understandable given what these anxieties can become if they occupy the center stage of immediate experience. Dread, panic, and terror are all accurate words for the feeling prompted by an immediate and full head-on, eye-to-eye, conscious experience of the unknowns of life and death.

Such thoughts are quite disturbing. We have what Paul Tillich, in his book *The Courage To Be*, has called "fate anxiety." That is, we have anxiety about what will become of us, what will happen to us, and how will it happen. We wish it would be wonderful but fear it will be terrible. In the same book Tillich elaborates on other anxieties that come with human existence. I am indebted to his work for my discussion of these anxieties.

Death Anxiety

Most obvious with regard to the anxieties of human existence is our anxiety about the fact that we cease to exist. We will die. Before any thoughts about an afterlife prompt an objection to this statement, let me clarify what I mean by saying, "We will die." I simply mean that we will cease to exist as we do now and that while we may have many beliefs about what is to come, we do not know of it experientially as we do when we, for example, travel to Paris by plane and then return home to tell about it. Whatever happens to us at death, none of us has ever been completely through it and come back again so that we know it experientially. None of us can say that we've been there and know what it's all about. Thus, whatever else it may be, the experience of dying itself and the state of death or that which follows is unknown to us by our own experience.

It is possible that we cannot even imagine non-being or non-existence. Sigmund Freud wrote at one time in his life that there was nothing in our being that was willing to consider death (as in the complete end of our existence). I wonder how many of us would believe in God if there was no hope of an afterlife attached to belief in God. Yet, if we loved God more than we love ourselves, it seems that we would be willing to be devoted to that God whether some form of our own continued existence is offered or not.

Even with an afterlife we do not know the exact nature of it. Do we have a consciousness at all similar to our present state? Are we separate individuals in this consciousness? Even if life does not cease in all ways, the life as we have known it does and we have no reports covering the minute details of what the "hereafter" is like. Finally, if there is an afterlife in the form of a paradise that not every soul will pass into, how "narrow is the gate"? This has been a source of death anxiety for many among the faithful. It is clear that we can and do have anxiety, at least as an undercurrent in the background of our emotional lives about what will or will not happen to us in life and in death. We defend against the dread, terror, and panic that is aroused by realizing the disasters that might strike us or those we love. Sudden unforeseen disasters that would leave us or them impoverished, destitute, financially ruined, maimed, in constant pain, or mentally debilitated, we put out of our conscious minds most of the time.

Life Anxiety

A prominent fear of our time is of becoming demented or insane. We can think of little worse than "going crazy." There is now a psychiatric diagnosis of "panic disorder." The symptoms include, among other things, the acute fears of "going crazy" and of dying. In such attacks, the defenses ordinarily used to ward off these various existential anxieties "leak" and allow a fuller force of these

15

anxieties into conscious awareness, often following periods of stress, fatigue, and exhaustion or inner conflict concerning a major decision or change. What leaks through, it is arguable, is not just the imagination gone wild due to hyper-arousal. Rather, there is an acute emotional recognition of the realities of human existence — that we will die and that we might lose our mental capacities. This sense of "doom" from an existential perspective is not at all imaginary or delusional.

Feelings of emptiness, loneliness, or incompetence lurk for many as a fate worse than death. The writings of some current psychoanalysts and psychiatrists such as Otto Kernberg describe such feelings as components of psychopathology. Many otherwise well-functioning people experience these feelings to a poignant if not a worse-than-death degree. The assumptions behind the pathologizing of these feeling states include the belief that the healthy, whole self feels quite well as an autonomous self, separated and individuated from others. It is also a question whether such a sense of extreme autonomy is not itself built on a denial of the realities of existence and the utilization of an egoistic defense against them.

Fears Of Meaninglessness

Another cause of anxiety is the sense that our lives are meaningless, that there is nothing of significant consequence from, or during, our lives. It is true that this may be viewed as a type of anxiety about our fate. However, for many the fate of a life that is felt to be meaningless is a fate worse than death. Thus, many will give their life in the service of a cause that will provide a sense of meaning and many will die for a cause that will give a meaning to their life by sacrificing it in death. At some level it is felt that achieving such a meaning allows one to outlive the self since the meaning or the cause lives on after the individual life is gone. Ernest Becker in his book *The Denial Of Death* has elegantly discussed the psychological mechanics of such acts of "heroism."

16

Identification, Fear, And Guilt

Of course, such fears may arise in the context of whatever ethical codes and religious and moral beliefs we have. Even apart from such beliefs it seems that we can become anxious by identifying with others. We think that what has just happened to them might happen to us. The fact that it did happen to someone and we saw it makes this more undeniably real. By this process of identification we can be traumatized by watching another suffer. This is especially true if we witness bodily assault with obvious and massive physical damage or death. Thus, when we conclude that we have been the cause of the sufferings of another person we sense something akin to guilt because we, in part, identify with the victim. We try to make the victims not like us, but we know somewhere in ourselves that they are like us. Knowing that someone might cause us a similar injury, this identification may turn unconscious guilt into fear. If this awareness is coupled with the knowledge that we were the cause of the harm and particularly if that harm was intentional, we will experience some form of guilt or fear based on identification with the victim at some level. This guilt and fear has been reported even by professional killers in interviews published by news magazines.

The guilt may be displaced onto something such as the fear of one's own death. Conscience, at least with regard to harming others, may be less the product of learning than we have thought. Harming another may have an inescapable psychological consequence, though we resist the thought that we may be "wired" that way. At the very least, I will probably want to believe the person harmed was not like me or somehow deserved it. This, of course, leads to feeling separated from this "other." At some point we will have defined so many people that we have harmed as "not like me" that feelings of alienation from others in general will occur as a result.

Fears Of Not Being All That We Might Be

Yet another aspect of our human condition that can arouse anxiety if they are not named are anxieties about feelings of a "moral" nature, feelings of guilt, and feelings of inadequacy. These are not

17

only feelings that we have done something wrong, but also fears that we have not done all that we might have done. Given that our imagination permits us to envision so many wonderful possibilities, few if any of us have done or become all that we have imagined. This results in a recognized discrepancy between what is and what might have been that can be painful. As creatures with imaginations that can project forward in time; as beings with memory, some sense of loss about not actualizing all that we believe we might have been or have done is almost inevitable.

As we name the anxieties they become more like fears. However, since these causes are more abstract than concrete and are thus quite vague, it seems more accurate to call them anxieties. Related to the moral and guilt-focused anxieties are our concerns about our inadequacy or helplessness to do that which we think we should do or should be able to do even if we appear most unable to do it. We may feel we should be able to alter the course of our existence or someone else's. We may feel that we should be able to rescue ourselves and/or others from some type of misery even if the others and parts of ourselves do not wish to be "rescued" or changed. Some may feel inadequate and unable to do that which appears possible in the eyes of many. Discerning the difference between what can be done and what cannot be done is often our greatest problem, and it is resolved only in the attempt to do it.

Likewise, I can experience anxiety and fear concerning my inadequacy to alter the other anxieties with regard to feelings of guilt, feelings of meaninglessness, emptiness, and loneliness as well as anxiety about the death of myself or another. In other words, I can become even more anxious due to my sense of inadequacy and helplessness or impotence to stop all these other anxieties. Even if I cannot alter the particulars of how human life itself appears to be constructed with certain givens and certain limits, I can feel that I should be able to do so. This anxiety concerning limits and our inadequacies may be, nevertheless, more comfortable than accepting that there are, in fact, such givens and limits. We strongly resist this conclusion.

Avoiding Painful Awareness

We wish to avoid pain in life, but then it seems that, given the eventual death of ourselves and all others coupled with all the other risks in life that may lead to serious loss and emotional pain, the indefinite avoidance of pain is impossible. This knowledge alone gives a certain pain that anticipates the possibilities and eventualities of life. Consequently, this is a knowledge that we try very hard not to know about. A conscious attempt to "not know" only makes us all the more aware of these quandaries of existence, just as trying not to think of pink elephants in the living room has a way of producing them in the mind. We try to ward off terror and dread and panic about life and death without being aware that this is what we are doing. Thus, we rarely look at these anxieties of existence straight on since they are under so many protective psychological layers of wrapping.

Only when there is a major intrusion into consciousness of a highly charged emotional nature, such as a serious automobile accident or other crisis, do we reckon in earnest with the bedrock matters of our existence. When we feel that we cannot do otherwise then we will look that which may seem evil in the eye. When we are terrified, then we will listen to what "the devil has to say." Only when hanging on the edge of the cliff do we see that the terror of pursuing demons offsets the terror of the abyss. Only when we realize that we have no choice will we allow ourselves to truly acknowledge what we are up against. This avoidance is tragic because the moment of reckoning is put off and deferred indefinitely until some crisis occurs. Yet the realizations from such a crisis and the navigation through it can change the course of life thereafter for the better as well as for the worse. For fear of the moment, we would rather not know the outcome and we defer the time of reckoning. Perhaps we are afraid of the worst. As we sit, we defer the reckoning as if in compartments on a train passing the time. We smoke our cigarettes, have a beer, share jokes and stories, or read the daily news and catch up on some work, never once thinking about the fact that we have been told that the train is speeding toward an eventual cliff, from which it will fall and tumble end over end over end into the absolute darkness of never-ending space.

On such a ride if someone whispered to you that he had some ideas about how to manage the rest of the ride and the fall, would you wish to hear it? Probably not, at least not until the part of the train with you on it had begun to fall. Then the terror of falling might override the terror of listening. So it is with our fears about life and death. Nevertheless, those who have been pushed from the cliff, tumbled a ways but then landed on a ledge before another eventual fall into space, may have the urge to create, in some way, something out of the experience of the fall. Perhaps it is just to ward off fears of meaninglessness and helplessness or perhaps it is an attempt at some sort of "rescue" in one way or another of the train riders. Most likely it is a mixture of these and other motives.

Inner Conflict As A Vice

On one side of our position in existence are our inner fears and anxieties. On the other side are our wishes and desires. Together both sides amount to an "inner vice" of sorts holding us in our human condition. Given that our desires arise from within us, we usually think of satisfying them instead of holding them at bay as we do our anxieties and fears, which we usually think of as originating from external threats. Yet death is eventually from within us if it is not from somewhere else first. Likewise, our desires, while originating within us, generally have as their goal something outside of the self. It is, therefore, fair to say that the vice seems cosmic because it is inescapable and it is inescapable because it is by and large within us — within the human organism in its natural condition and context. It is the very fact that the cosmic vice is within us and is therefore inescapable that drives us to despair about our human situation. Therefore, we run and try to hide from the realization that it is, in fact, within us, a part of our human nature as far as we know it.

Within us we have not only the desire to satisfy the physical necessities to maintain life, but also the emotional desires for more than enough of all of these things. It is as if we somehow want to be absolutely sure we will have enough. Here desire and fear may coincide since the emotional desire to have more may be a function of the fear that we will not have enough. We want more than enough and we then become greedy. We desire other emotional satisfactions also so that we may never feel adequately satisfied. We want more of most every material good. We want better than we have had, better than others have, and better than we have ever known of existing. Many of us desire power and influence over others. We fear that if we don't have the power, someone else will have it and we fear what will happen to us then. Alternatively, we may long to be taken care of and to be nurtured as if there could never be enough, or we wish to be catered to and admired to the point of being worshiped although we may call it being "loved." Prestige and social status are desires whose stomachs are bottomless pits. We may desire to be smart, creative, and good too, but this is usually intertwined with what we desire others to think of us. Perhaps it is more accurate to note that the wish for others to think well of us is the primary desire. Of course, we want to think well of ourselves too. Most of these emotional desires can take the form of a sexual expression, which may be a part of why sexual desire in humans extends well beyond the satisfaction of a biological drive.

The attempt to satisfy desires after the basic physical needs of life have been satisfied may serve the function of warding off fears. However, wishes and fears may have an antagonistic relationship such that while I wish for one thing, say a promotion at work, I also fear another thing if the wish comes true. For example, if I get the promotion I'll get more responsibility and I may not be sure I want that. So I compromise (but not consciously in all likelihood) and only half-heartedly pursue the promotion. Then when I don't get it I'm angry at myself or the boss, whereas if I had admitted that I wasn't sure I wanted the promotion, I could have just not bothered with it at all. However, then I would have to be willing to accept any criticism I might receive for not wanting the promotion. Conflicts between wishes and fears, in which a part of the self wishes to approach something and a part wishes to avoid it, create a tension within us by virtue of there being two opposing forces at work. If we cannot make a conscious compromise then we may make a compromise outside of our awareness. This type of compromise usually lets us avoid deciding to do something one way or

21

another and often exacts its own toll for letting us off the hook with regard to a tough decision. These compromises made "under the table" can be viewed as causing "symptoms" or other problems which are frequently the presenting complaint when coming to see a mental health professional, a physician, or a member of the clergy.

Avoidance

There is a picture in my old introductory psychology book of a little boy reaching to pet a goose, but just a few inches from the goose he froze in space, apparently realizing that the goose might bite him. At the moment the picture was taken the little boy apparently couldn't move toward the goose to pet it for fear of being bitten, but neither could he just abandon his desire to pet the goose and walk away from it. He was stuck at an impasse as we are too with many of our greatest dilemmas. We approach what our desires tell us we want, but then, before grasping it, we are halted by fear.

Frequently this fear and our halting a pursuit is a good thing given the possible consequences of continuing to go after whatever we desire. At this point, a part of the mind may wish to have a belief in a God such that this belief would somehow contain the anxieties inherent in us that we have looked at. But then another part of the mind fears that such a belief may be in error and that it would cause us to miss something, even if only not to know what part of us imagines might be "the truth." We may also fear what this God might do or expect us to do. We would reach toward God as the little boy would reach to pet the goose, but then draw back when we suspect that something frightening might happen, just as the boy feared the goose would bite him.

Living with fears and desires that bolster each other is distressing enough as it is, but having fears and desires that conflict can make for greater agony. We know we could get out of these inner vices if only we would either overcome our fears or abandon our desires, but often we feel unable to do either. Stuck at these impasses we sense an irritation if not an anger at ourselves for feeling so unable. It seems at the time that life without what we want or with what we fear would be unbearable. We conclude that we couldn't, shouldn't, and therefore won't tolerate either having the pain or losing the pleasure that comes with a decision to resolve the impasse. We refuse to believe that we can't have it all and so we will let go of nothing that promises what seems to be an essential pleasure and we will hold onto nothing that causes pain unless it somehow also promises an even greater pleasure.

This then is the problem. We are trapped by the insatiability of our desires, by the fact that our desires conflict, and by the fears attached to getting what we think we want. We are also trapped by the frustration that such a position causes since it makes a loss of some kind inevitable. We are trapped in knowing that we will lose our own life here as we know it including our relationships as they are now, that our lives may seem lacking in meaningfulness, and that we feel some desire to manage or control matters in a way that resembles how perfectly we imagine things might be. Yet this way eludes us. Concerning all of these we may sense loss, frustration, and despair, which in turn may give rise to the inclination to be aggressive at times to the point of being destructive in order to assert some power. We are also challenged in our human condition to absorb loss, anxiety, fear, frustration, and despair and to contain destructive aggression. The following discussion examines how we might respond to the human condition described.

Chapter 2

Managing Our
Frustrations, Losses, And Fears

Managing By Satisfying Desires

Sigmund Freud postulated that once we realize we can never cease desiring nor satisfy all of our desires, we want to cease existing. This "death instinct" or "death wish" is simply the wish to die when the futility of life is fully realized. Freud never developed an adequate counterbalance or resolution to the death instinct although he had originally thought that the "life instinct," all the forces acting to preserve life and experience including sexuality and procreation, would neutralize the death wish. One analyst summed it up this way: "All the organism wants is to stop wanting." Thus, finally one of our desires becomes the desire to stop desiring. At this point we realize that our desires can own us instead of vice-versa.

There is an old tale of "The Chinese Monkey Trap." In China there is said to be a particular type of monkey that can be trapped by putting food in a heavy jar with a long, narrow neck. The neck is so narrow that once the monkey has reached in and filled its fist with food, the full fist cannot pass back through the neck of the jar. Although he cannot actually eat the food, the monkey will not let go of the food to regain his freedom even when the trappers who set the jar up come to capture him. The monkey has been trapped by his own desires. When we realize that we can be or are trapped by our own desires we may wish to escape them even if the escape is by death.

The acute recognition of our state of endless desire and fear, our passions and our anxieties, can lead us to despair when we see how little we can do about them and what the real options are. If we stop short of a despair that longs for death we may attempt to deaden our anxiety by dulling the senses with alcohol or other drugs. This in turn promotes desire for and dependency on the substance that helps us avoid despair or anxiety and so we may develop an addiction. If we do not deaden our consciousness to our condition we can distract ourselves from it with endless pastimes of work, relationships, and leisure. These may become habits, even addictions, themselves. We can become very dependent on anything that helps us avoid the anxiety or other emotional discomfort that we would otherwise feel. Interestingly, some of these distractions cause us to flirt quite closely with the very anxieties we wish to avoid. For example, the pastimes of smoking and motorcycle racing distract our conscious minds from other thoughts with an act that actually increases our risk of an earlier death and a painful one at that. It might be said such activities help to convince us that we can defy death by flirting with it. Then we develop by way of a habit the desire for something that causes a risk of the death we fear. Undoubtedly these activities can be interpreted equally well in other ways. Obviously, denial, the defense of the ostrich putting its head in the sand as if to say whatever is feared just isn't there, is alive and well with human beings too.

Disconnecting the sense of self from experience is also a way of coping with the human position in life. That is, saying to ourselves, "This isn't really happening to me — it's just my body," or something to this effect, whereas in denial we say, "This isn't really happening." By the use of such defenses we attempt to hide our fearful self and our desirous self from the rest of our self by, in one way or another, shrinking it, glossing over it, or walling it off.

Managing By Merging

Two other solutions for dealing with our anxiety are described by Earnest Becker in *The Denial Of Death* as "the twin ontological motives." One of these is the merging of the individual self with a group so that it is the group that defines our meaning for us and how to achieve it. The individual merges the sense of self with the group even to the point of the sacrifice of the self for what the group considers important. The self is then lost in the group but the person believes there is a chance of cheating death by living in the mind and memory of the group if sufficiently heroic acts are done. Becker writes that this sense of merger of the self with the group rests on what he calls the "transference solution" because using it

26

we look to some larger "other" to define what is meaningful for us. Then we undertake the living out of the wishes of the other, in essence to get their approval, possibly to the point of becoming a "hero."

Although the other is most often a collective group such as a nation, political party, or family, it may also be an individual, such as in the case of romantic love. In this type of romance the other is highly idealized, even "worshiped." The devotee is thrilled to please his or her idealized one and finds meaning in life both in the presence of the other and through an approval which the admirer/devotee hopes will eventually grow into a reciprocation of the idealization resulting in a state of mutual adoration.

The idealization or the holding of some reverence for and sense of awe of the other is key here because it is that which gives the other the power to transform the devoted one's sense of self. It is the idealization that permits the other to appear larger than life and thus offer the possibility of transformation of the devotee into a larger-than-life being too. This process also takes the sting out of death, since the death takes on lasting, even seemingly eternal, significance. According to Becker, this transference solution, the idealization of the other, is the driving force behind acts of heroism in battle and sacrifices of the self for some group or individual since the "hero" is, in great part, becoming heroic to achieve the larger-than-life status in the eyes of the other. Thus the hero in some sense feels he/she will live on even if only in the memory of the group. This explanation of self-sacrificial acts is so limited that it appears inadequate to explain something so complex by itself.

Before going further we should recall that Freud originally "discovered" transference as a phenomenon arising in the process of psychoanalysis such that the patient showed an overestimation of the powers of the analyst. The patient came to feel the analyst was larger than life and could fulfill the patient's wishes to make the patient's fears go away somehow in much the same way a parent might do for a young child when, for example, coming into the child's dark bedroom at night and pronouncing everything to be safe. The parent can also kiss a young child's bruise and make the pain go away. This can be done not only because the child wishes for it to be so, but also because the child as a child does not question the parent's power nor think, "This is just suggestion. Nothing has really changed." The child at this age believes that the parent really can make the pain go away in addition to wishing it to be so. The child has "faith" in the parent's ability and needs this faith as a part of the felt dependency upon the parent. Transference was originally thought of as the wish for this benign, protective parent of childhood to be found again somewhere else. Thus, the patient in psychoanalysis was seen to be "transferring" wishes for the powerful but kind parent of childhood onto the analyst. This brings us right back to desire again.

Becker expands on the original psychoanalytic understanding of transference to say that it is universal. It is not just in psychoanalysis that we bring forward into adulthood our wishes for a benign, protective other who can by his/her mere presence make everything feel good again. The problem with attempting the transference solution is that it requires one to remain a dependent child who sees the other as uniquely potent. This is to abdicate adulthood and relationships between equals insofar as the transference is directed toward other people. A romance is unlikely to last if built upon such a one-sided idealization; the idealized one will most often eventually feel lonely and without adult company. Indeed, that will be the case because the adoring one has tacitly bargained to remain a child. Nevertheless, Becker's emphasis on the universality of the transference wish is of great significance. We will return to the issue of transference again but first let us consider the other solution for our anxiety regarding life and death discussed by Becker.

Managing By Enlarging The Sense Of Self

Becker's other "motive" or means of dealing with the basic anxieties of life and death is the development of the autonomous or independent self. Instead of losing the self in some "other," more experience is sought to heighten the sense of the self in order to believe in its autonomy, potency, and self-sufficiency to navigate the course through life and all that arises alone. It seems that this is in essence an attempt to enlarge the sense of the self to the point of feeling invincible. If one believes he/she will in fact dismiss the realities prompting life and death anxiety, then the sense of self has bordered on being, if it has not already become, grandiose. From another perspective such a person is living in a state of denial since all people face the same realities of death and possible sudden disaster. Some, by virtue of their present condition at this moment or in the past, can convince themselves that they are beyond the reach of threat, disaster, ruin, and despair. This may become denial to the point of delusion. Yet this is what the solution of the autonomous self rests on. Although it may not be acknowledged, the defense of self-enlargement results eventually in an even more grandiose, self-centered sense of self or a narcissism of sorts because it also rests on an over-estimation of the self resulting in an idealization of the self, some self-part, or some extension of the self such as one's children or work. The solution of self-enlargement may defend adequately against some of the anxieties of life and death. However, it cannot defend indefinitely against the very desires it thrives upon because eventually a loss of some kind will occur. This brings us back to the self-destructive aspect of Freud's death wish. When one realizes that the desires requiring satisfaction to continue the enlargement of the self are endless and that they are often conflicting, then a sense of frustration with the self emerges which can result in aggression against the self in order to cease existence and the sense of frustration, emptiness, despair, or anxiety.

The continuous enlargement of the self requires that the self not engage in any idealization of another being. More importantly, however, the defense of self-enlargement, if seen as sufficient, ignores that the desires of the self will in all likelihood come into conflict with each other at some time. For example, if at the same moment in time I desire both the freedom to pursue new adventures in romance and to enter a monogamous marriage with a particular woman whom I will lose if I do not, then I must choose between my desires and giving something up. With such a decision I experience a defeat in the acquisition of all that the autonomous, ever-enlarging self desires. I also will probably experience extreme anxiety at the loss of an aspect of myself that I then believe is essential to my meaning in life. A mini-death of sorts will occur at the sacrifice of this part of my self-system. As is evident from this situation, conflicting desires give rise to anxiety concerning the unknowns of what the loss inherent in any major choice between two or more possibilities will bring.

Conflict, Decisions, And Loss

We are only truly able to make decisions requiring a choice when we are able to leave all other doors closed and unentered as we open one door and enter in. To carry this a step further with the marital choice dilemma, I might think that I will marry the woman and maintain the pretense of monogamy while then keeping extra-marital ventures a secret. I have then made the choice to make a barrier between myself and my spouse, the barrier of a major secret that I know and cannot share. With this act I have chosen to compromise my intimacy and honesty with my spouse and I have lost it because of my choice. If she discovers what I have done she will at least see me differently and then I have lost something else I desire — to be held in her high regard. These are corners in life from which there is no escape without a loss. Nevertheless, we do not wish to admit it to ourselves and therefore we continue to act as if we can have it both ways and satisfy all of our desires.

We wish to avoid the recognition of these binds because they force us to reckon with our limitations. We do not wish to see that there are limits to the satisfaction of desire inherent in how human beings are constructed and limits to the satisfaction of desire built into the real situations in which we live. We do not wish to see these limits because we wish to keep the satisfaction of our desires as our purpose in life. Admitting the limits of the satisfaction of desire may cause us anxiety or despair.

Instead of looking only at our inner vice simply as fears conflicting with desires or mutually conflicting desires, we can be quite accurate and expand our picture to include both mutually conflicting desires and their related mutually conflicting fears. In such a situation we might have a person who engages in a life-threatening activity repeatedly, such as having unprotected sexual intercourse with relative strangers. He desires to do this because of the thrill of the adventure as well as the sexual gratification. Yet he also fears the act because of the risk of contracting the AIDS virus. This fear is associated with a part of him that desires to give this behavior up, but he fears that if he does he will become bored and his life will feel empty and meaningless. Further, the biochemistry of excitement is such that it can cause addiction to whatever we choose as a source of excitement or arousal. Consequently, these choices need to be made with the understanding that we are forming and increasing the attachment to whatever the exciting act is. The same is true concerning whatever is chosen as a means to reduce anxiety and tension. The likelihood of its further use increases each time it is used. A habit or addiction can develop with any thing or act that is used to create excitement, a pleasurable state, or to decrease or avoid anxiety, fear, and unpleasant states.

Consider something a bit more ordinary such as a forty-year-old man who desires a promotion at work. While he desires it and what the increased salary will allow as well as the prestige of the advancement in the company, he simultaneously fears he will lose his colleagues as friends if he becomes their supervisor. This, coupled with the added responsibility and additional hours per week of work, prompt him to fear being promoted. Nevertheless, he also fears that if he is not promoted, he will be viewed by his family and neighbors as a failure and as foolish for staying with the company because he was not given a promotion, even though he enjoys his work there.

Consider a woman whose first child died and she desires another. She fears that if she has a second, that child may die also. Her fears are manifold. She is afraid that she will be a poor mother if she has a child, and she is afraid that she will be lonely when she is old if she doesn't have another child. She fears she will then regret that decision for the rest of her life.

People with inner conflicts such as these exist in almost every house on your street and not just in the psychotherapist's office. Most of us have some such quandaries. We defend against feeling the acute emotions associated with them by any number of methods. It seems apparent that we ensnare ourselves with our wishes and our fears, our desires and our anxieties. It is from ourselves that we wish to escape but cannot escape.

Our Introduction To Pain And Pleasure

To delve more deeply into the complexities of our state beyond describing the inner vice in which we exist with our conflicting desires and conflicting fears on each side of the vice, we must look at the human infant immediately following birth. The human infant is born into this world with the "hardwiring" in its biology to respond to food and nurturing attention with feelings of pleasure, and to the lack of food and nurturing attention as well as other frustrations with displeasure or pain. In fact, when an infant is in what we would call a frustrating situation it complains with loud crying. Then, if not gratified, he appears angry if not enraged. The infant is born, in almost all instances, into a situation that will provide the opportunity for both sets of feelings, since the baby will be fed and cuddled sometimes but not immediately whenever it is wished for. The human infant gains experience with gratification and pleasure which promote feelings of love, attachment, and a sense of oneness with the caretaker. Likewise, the human infant eventually gains experience with frustration, that is, with the experience of the delay if not the withholding of the food and nurturance that it wants. This frustration by all appearances prompts anger and rage. A series of psychology experiments done many years ago established what is called "the frustration-aggression hypothesis." This simply states that when a human being is frustrated with regard to the satisfaction of a need or perhaps simply a desire or a wish, it is more likely to become aggressive.

The human infant comes into the world ready by predisposition to respond in these ways. The situations that will "pull for" or trigger both of these responses are inherent in the way this world exists. Therefore, the infant cannot escape these opposing emotional experiences. This process has been described by many as having these phenomena. The state induced is called "splitting," as it entails the infant's experiencing the caretaker at times as being "all good," perfect, and gratifying and at other times being sensed as "all bad," depriving, withholding, and destructive. It has been concluded that in order for the infant to move into toddlerhood and see itself as psychologically separate from the caretaker, the conflicting "all good" and "all bad" images in the child's mind must be integrated or mended to form a more constant whole. This requires a binding of the rage and aggression felt towards the depriving other with the love felt towards the gratifying other by "realizing" emotionally that they are one and the same person. This leads to more balanced and realistic feelings toward the caretaker.

These two sets of feelings — pleasure and attachment on the one hand and pain and rage on the other — become the cores around which other later experiences cluster. Therefore, painful or "bad" experiences tend to be associated with prior painful, bad experiences. They may activate the cumulative rage stored in the emotional or bodily memory associated with prior frustrations. Likewise, pleasurable, "good" experiences tend to be associated with and activate the feelings that occurred with prior gratifying experiences. These good feelings promote the expression of attachment and affection while the bad feelings when activated may push for the expression of rage, hostility, and aggression. Further, whatever or whoever the unintegrated feelings get directed towards may be sensed by the infant and later the child as either ideal, wonderful, and perfect, or as worthless, horrible, or evil.

From our earliest days, then, we have, as a function of how we are made, two basic dispositions and sets of feelings that we can associate with any thing, person, or event that comes into our experience. Watching little children at play, especially those less than three years old, will provide all of the evidence for this that is necessary. These two clusters of emotion may represent the cores of what Freud called the life instinct and the death instinct. All feeling that works toward perpetuating attachment, cooperation, and the survival of humanity, and that rests on a felt sense of oneness or merging to some degree with each other, might be viewed as springing from the life instinct. All feeling that works toward death, destruction, and against maintaining relationships with others might be viewed as springing from the death instinct.

From the description of these clusters of emotion and their associated behaviors, it appears that they can also be related in part to Becker's conception of merger with another versus the autonomous self. The merger clearly relates to the cluster containing feelings of attachment to and pleasure with others. Actually, Becker calls it the "*agape* merger." However, I would like to reserve the term and concept of *agape* and use it in a more restricted way that I believe is more accurate.

Becker's autonomous self by its definition pushes toward separation from others. Moreover, movement towards the autonomous self would seem also to set the wishes and desires of the self above those of the larger group, society, or culture. In doing this the autonomous self assumes the prerogative of imposing its desires on others, if by way of nothing else then by way of imposing the separation of itself onto the other even if that separation in some way harms the other. It appears that the autonomous self would move rapidly toward treating others as objects if it does not in fact begin from such a position. The autonomous self has decided to maximize its potential to experience and possibly to acquire or to dominate. Of course, this does not necessarily lead to a destructive rage being inflicted on others. Yet it seems fair to say that the autonomous self may experience the desires of others that would impede this maximizing of its potential as frustrating.

If all people were similarly autonomous, the degree of societal unity would be minimal. This in no way suggests that every society does not need its autonomous selves. It is to propose that the self, autonomous from the group, may be or may become narcissistic. Such a narcissism would include a sense of entitlement to that which is desired. Ultimately such narcissism is an inadequate defense against the potential despair resulting from our position in existence — our human situation as described here. The defense of the autonomous self is inadequate because it rests on the satisfaction of its own desires as the provider of meaning for life and death. To believe that these desires will not conflict with each other in any significant way resulting in a loss or deprivation of something is to be in a state of denial to the point of seeing oneself as different from the rest of humanity. Since, in all likelihood, everyone at some time will have a dilemma like the "to marry" or "not to marry" dilemma, in which one of the desires will go unsatisfied because they are mutually exclusive, all desires cannot be satisfied simultaneously. Frustrations and disappointments due to loss will exist and thus, if the meaning to my life is only to avoid frustration, I

34

will never be able to achieve it fully. For the autonomous self to be completely self-sufficient it would mean that such a person would never direct outwardly his/her experience of anxiety, despair, or grief, in response to the satisfaction of the desires being unattainable. In other words, the autonomous self would have to believe that it is uniquely able to defend against the anxiety inherent in human existence alone and somehow not have conflicting desires that require a solution outside of the self. The existential writers, such as Camus and Sartre, who focus on what appears to amount to the autonomous self, seem to be acutely aware of the experience of these anxieties. However, at least one other possibility appears even more compelling than this in addressing why the defense of the autonomous self is inadequate to master the potential anxieties and despair of human life and death.

In order to pursue this possibility we must return to our two opposing clusters of experience and feeling. The feeling cluster of attachment to that which is sensed as pleasurable and wonderful might be understood as the origin of what has been previously defined as transference. This state would today be specified as that of a "positive" transference. Likewise, the feeling state associated with pain, deprivation, and rage would be understood as the effect of "negative" transference. These two feeling states, though in varying degrees of intensity, are to some extent waiting to be activated and transferred toward whatever or whoever comes along. If this occurs outside of psychotherapy, it would be more correct to call them transference-like feelings or perhaps transferential feelings. They are identifiable as transferential feelings when the degree of positive or negative emotion or corresponding behavior is disproportionate to what most would see as warranted by the particular triggering event occurring at the moment. The trigger at the moment brings forward a multitude of feelings associated with other experiences that have been stored up and that flow forward once there is an adequate trigger to prompt them.

Becker's observation that transference (of the positive type) is universal is most significant as it suggests that we all have the tendency to want some idealized other to protect us and take care of us like a good parent. As Becker notes, we are then wishing for something like a deity or God. We desire the activation of the positive emotional feeling cluster and fear the activation of the negative emotional feeling cluster.

The goal of humankind in one way or another has always been for the positive state to be victorious over the negative state. In some religions it is hoped that God will triumph over the devil or at least that good will triumph over evil. Early psychoanalysts hoped for the life instinct to contain or control the death instinct. Later psychotherapies have hoped for love to bind and contain hate and attachment to supersede aggression. Often the fantasy has been for the total obliteration of pain and aggression as is implied, albeit not always directly expressed, in the optimism of some humanistic psychology.

Many, if not most, of these systems of thought have denied that pain and frustration will always be a part of human existence as far as can be foreseen due, if nothing else, to the inevitability of death. While psychoanalysis and existentialism did not ignore the dark side of the human being, the picture painted was so pessimistic that it offered little, if any, hope for the betterment of humanity. The psychoanalytic solution of the renunciation of infantile wishes has seemed little better to many than one Buddhist solution which calls for the death of desire. Both can appear by the description to be devoid of the hope, optimism, and joy that human beings, for good reason, resist giving up.

Given the cluster of feelings that wishes for the self to attach to something or someone it can adore, something in each life will assume a god-like position. It will be whatever or whomever we value most and the thing or person through which we obtain our meaning for life. Therefore, it also will be associated with our defenses against the basic anxieties around life and death. We will idealize it and therefore grant this thing or person a considerable measure of power and influence over us. All of this is done in an effort of the self to protect itself from the existential anxieties including the fears that the self may be destroyed, that the self is bad or evil, and the fear that the self may destroy itself or feel poorly either for being bad or inadequate. So in agreement with Becker, but said differently, we will need to idealize something.

Now the autonomous self and the merger with the other do not appear so divergent. Both rest on the idealization of something, be it the group, a particular other such as in romance, or the self. So idealization is a common denominator. We will then idealize something. We will turn to something or someone with our anxiety, desire, and despair; we will believe that whatever or whoever it is can help us. It may be a spouse. It may be alcohol. It may be the part of ourselves that we see as "rational," "intuitive," "worldly wise," "cool," or "good." However, none of these can maintain the appearance of perfection indefinitely to one who retains a critical eye. All will eventually disappoint, for nothing on this earth is perfect. Nor is it always gratifying when gratification is wanted. Particularly if it is the self which is idealized, there is a problem. The self knows itself not to be perfect in some part of the mind that has access to its fears and insatiable desires. At this point the psyche knows itself to be vulnerable because it is in a state of inner conflict. The only being or thing capable of actually being perfect and therefore of continuing to appear perfect to us is something divine, something like God. Yet if we acknowledge that a deity or God is or even might be there, often we are not sure how perfect it is. The existence of what we see as "evil" may make believing in our all-good and all-powerful deity difficult and, for some, seemingly impossible. The existence of perceived evil is perhaps the biggest obstacle to a belief in a divine being. Apparent evil can then block our search for the ideal from having a spiritual focus and resolution.

Anxiety And Desire That Result In Evil

Much that we most probably would consider evil — aggression that leads to death and destruction which springs from humans — is the result of attempts in some way to protect or defend that which we idealize or believe to be most valuable. We feel we must engage in such protective acts or our meaning in life is at risk. It is through that which we idealize, that toward which we live in a state of positive transference, that onto which we project our hopes for mastering life and in some way or another of defeating death, that we find our meaning. Becker describes acts of self-sacrifice for the other through which we find meaning as attempts at heroism. This seems accurate since the hero is alive in the group's memory. However, a deeper understanding of idealization as an aspect of our beliefs or defenses that assist in managing our pains due to loss and our life and death anxiety, will help us respond constructively to these anxieties. Such a constructive response would be less prone to result in the death and destruction we see as evil.

Nevertheless, it appears that we must look at the larger category of our fears and desires in order to grasp the essence of evil as caused by human beings. Protecting and defending that which we idealize can, in fact, result in a variation of evil springing from our desires and fears. Our idealizations serve to protect us from our fears and assist us in gratifying our desires so we will direct this inclination or wish toward something. If we idealize nothing else we may tend to idealize or value most highly the gratification of our most basic drives and desires — hunger, thirst, sleep, and sex — in that we would then live primarily for their satisfaction. Alternatively, we may hold the continuation of the experience of life itself or the avoidance of pain, as most valuable to us. In this case, it is the cessation of our experience of life or the onset of pain that we most fear. That which poses either a threat to the gratification of our desires or the activation of our fears frequently does trigger a state of frustration which can result in anger or rage as a consequence, since we feel as if nothing could be worse at that moment. That is to say, these threats elicit within us a state of negative transferential feelings toward the threat.

Obviously, as adults our rage is potentially much more destructive than the rage of the infant. Adult rage can and does often cause the death of the self or another. Suicide or any form of self-destructive act is still aggression simply with the self or a part of the self as its object. In order to protect the satisfaction of our desires, including the preservation of our idealizations, and to avoid pain, we destroy and kill. It is quite believable that this is the cause of and the essence of true "evil" as it is perpetuated by humankind. Death and destruction at the hands of human beings is brought about by the negative cluster of feelings, including fury and rage, being activated and directed toward some thing or some one we perceive as a threat to our continued life or the experience of pleasure or avoidance of pain in some form including the preservation of our idealizations. It appears that humans are made with the capacity for a primitive and powerful state of negative emotions. This capacity is so profound that to call it negative and transferential seems a ridiculous understatement. This might be thought of as aggression or fight for survival, and indeed it is. However, it seems fair to say that this mechanism activates the most potent negative emotions within us and permits them to be directed toward the source of the perceived threat. Admittedly, emotions fueling destructive behavior to preserve survival are not necessarily always negative. I use the term to indicate their destructive potential. The threat may be against that which seems vital to our self-interest, our desires, or simply against our self-interested desires broadly defined.

It would seem, then, that if this is the source of death, destruction, and misery or evil that is caused by humans, in order for evil to cease, human desire and fear must cease. This has been one Buddhist solution offered for life's problems. Insofar as the desires are primitive or "infantile," this is also much of the psychoanalytic solution. If we are not to abandon our desires or renounce our infantile desires, how can the evil we inflict be at least decreased if not totally contained?

Putting It Together

Human life includes "traps." Among them are that we will die, that we can worry about what will happen to us before we die, that we can imagine that life might be much more in some way or another than it is, and that we can be in a state of inner conflict about not only what we think but also how we feel about it. The anxiety, desire, despair, and frustration that arise from our human condition are at least sometimes uncomfortable. They are perhaps often most painful and we wish to avoid these feelings because they are so very disturbing. In order to avoid these feelings we may seek to numb our senses one way or another, or distract ourselves from them. We may "lose" ourselves by identifying closely (merging) with a group that we hold in highest esteem. We may accept an all-encompassing meaning in life found in association with or service to any and all individuals we are in awe of and idealize.

Alternatively, we can see a part of the self as that to which we turn in time of trouble, that which we value most highly and believe in most fully. We then idealize or sense as larger than life, an aspect of the self: the rational self, the creative self, the cunning self, the self that achieves, the self that is attractive, or the self that is "good." All are possibilities. Then internally, the troubled, pained self turns to another part of the self to be taken care of. But one way or another we will have some element of these feelings of anxiety or pain at some time and we direct them to something.

Chapter 3

The Transformation Of Desire
And Fear As The Solution
To The Human Condition

Reason And Emotion

Given what we have reviewed, in order for our frustration, despair, and resulting behavior that is either immediately or eventually destructive to be contained, a transformation of our anxieties including specific fears and our desires would seem necessary. Desire and fear would have to be transformed so that desire to have the absence of violence, destruction, and aggression that in turn results in suffering and death is greater than our desire for the possible gain by such aggression. Likewise, our fear of the activation of aggression must become greater than our fear of living without whatever we imagine such aggression would gain for us. We must fear the activation of a state of primitive fear that in turn provokes rage and the likelihood of aggression.

The solution of humanistic psychology at this juncture was that we should avoid pain and frustration for all. While the goal was good, this naive idealism ignored that the endless desires of many if not most people, when frustrated, would lead to aggression. It is not simply the frustration of the desires centered around our basic needs that may lead to aggression. It can be frustration due to the lack of gratification of a desire in people who believe they are entitled to whatever is wanted. The frustration of a person who feels "entitled" often triggers aggression. Overly autonomous and perhaps narcissistically-entitled individuals, who live apart from the constraint of accepting that their actions must not be destructive of others, pose the greatest threat of aggression and hence of evil. This is so because the more entitled one feels, the less one views anything else as equal in importance to the satisfaction of one's own desires. Destructive actions might also arise from the tension and anxiety generated by an acute sensing of one of the aspects of the human condition discussed earlier.

How could such a transformation of our desires come about? It seems quite unlikely that at this point in history we would all simultaneously decide and agree to change in this way. Yet this is what those who are idealistic with regard to our rational capacities have believed, especially since the rapid rise in popularity of the scientific method or "logical positivism" at the beginning of the twentieth century. This hope in the capacity of human reason denies that reasoning may well work in the service of our emotions and maintains that reason alone can and one day will control our emotions.

The poets and song writers have long said in a variety of ways that we see, hear, and think what we want or desire to see, hear, and think, and that we ignore the rest or we do not let it make sense to us. Our reasoning ability appears to be often more the agent of our desires and not vice-versa. If this were not so we would not find ourselves "addicted" to so many unreasonable things. We would calculate by reason alone who our best mate would be and we would realize that the cost of war in terms of human life is unreasonable in most cases, if not in all cases, and abandon it. We appear to have the ability to see why other people's wars are unreasonable or not worth the cost, but we never see our own wars as unreasonable, especially our personal "wars." Even when an insane man has come to power we send off large numbers of troops against troops instead of attempting to capture the leader and his inner circle, realizing that all the rest are under the spell of nationalism and are, as they see it, fighting for their country.

This is not an attempt to say that war is never the most reasonable option. That question is so large as to lead away from this discussion. The proposal is that our reasoning capacities will not alone contain our desires and our fears. The explanation for this must refer to the apparent insatiability of our desires and our lack of ability to become so passionate about being reasonable that it overcomes our other passions. We do not seem to be able to be so passionate about being reasonable that we abandon the destructive habits that the majority of us, if not all of us, now have.

42

Most of us are addicted to something. We have at least one compulsive habit that we cannot leave behind. This habit is costly and may be destructive. If nothing else, it uses resources including time and energy that if contained might be used for constructive, creative, beneficial purposes; instead the resources are consumed by the compulsion. This compulsion we cannot leave, in part because it distracts us from our primitive anxieties about life and death.

It would be reasonable to make some peace with these anxieties. But we will not because it is more comfortable to avoid thinking about them, and so our emotions dictate that we will be unreasonable and ignore vital matters because we are absorbed in and consumed by a compulsion. It may be a harmless pastime that is enjoyable or a "not so bad" habit. Such things as biting the fingernails, watching television for hours, obsessively looking for rare stamps, and endless preoccupation with the improvement of skill at something can all be compulsions and often are when we cannot leave them. Like the more dramatic situation of the alcoholic or drug addict, we say we could stop them if we wanted to but we don't wish to. With most of these activities we will never wish to stop them since they are of little or no consequence in terms of causing problems. Our choices then are not as rational as we would like to believe. Many diversions do escalate to the point that we harm ourselves or someone else.

Further, such diversions may dissipate our energy to create. We are creatures of pleasure enough that it seems unlikely we would sacrifice pleasure or endure frustration as the most reasonable choice in most situations. Rather, we want to use our reasoning to help us have still more pleasure. To use the popular formulation, we are "addicted" to the pursuit of our desires in general, whatever they may be.

If and when reason alone is able to contain "negative" emotions it appears to result in a joyless stoicism perhaps because of a despondency due to abandoning the pursuit of desire. Thus, even in situations where we force reason to prevail over emotion, we experience little satisfaction in this victory of reason, which is probably the bulk of why reason has so few victories over desire. Our

43

appetite for reasonability seems a bit less hungry than our other appetites. Finally, reason cannot triumph over emotion when we have conflicting desires and fears unless we are willing to lose something and to give something up. We are reluctant to do this. More often than not we will try to discover, by way of reason, a way to have all that we desire. Why do we find it so hard to eat less even when our stomachs are full? We know that to eat after being full is not reasonable. We engage in our habits beyond what we ourselves and others think is reasonable. In order for reason to triumph over emotion to a greater degree, some greater joy, pleasure, or happiness would have to be found by us in the triumph of reason.

The Divided Self

Despite habits bordering on, if not being, compulsions, one of the last things we wish to do is to admit that any of our actions are beyond our own control. This is a great offense to the part of us that wishes to be an autonomous self. It reveals the eventual and unavoidable defeat of the inflated sense of self as a defense because it points out that the self is not unified but is often divided. If the self is not a unified self with regard to a decision, one part of the self will suffer some degree of loss. It is because the self is an ambivalent self that it cannot achieve a victory as a self alone. Some part of the self will lose out if I want to marry Sally and I also want to marry Jane, or if I want to marry Sue and I also want to remain single to see who comes along. It is this ambivalent nature of the self that makes it impossible for us not to feel deprived or defeated whenever a decision is made that results in the choice of one thing over another. A part of the person wants to quit smoking and yet another part does not want to quit smoking. We have conflicting desires and only one can win out at any moment in time. If one part of the self wins in obtaining its desire, the other part loses in the getting of its desire, when those desires are conflicting.

Our desires are often conflicting. This is particularly so when one of these desires is to be reasonable and forego the satisfaction of the other. Restraint of desire for the sake of reason is made even more difficult when the desire is to destroy that which we believe is threatening us with loss including death, or the deprivation of

44

pleasure or a lack of meaningfulness in life. At this juncture we discover what might be described as the almost universal "addiction" to survival itself no matter what the cost or conditions, but survival and preferably under the best possible conditions.

Admittedly, it may appear to be complete nonsense to describe this as an addiction. Yet it is this which compels us, this from which we cannot escape, and this which at bedrock we are all but helpless to resist. We are nearly impotent with regard to the desire to keep our other desires, including those that prompt us to kill and destroy whatever threatens us, continuously in check. Ultimately, even if we were emotionally able, we do not wish to restrain these aggressive desires born of fear because, in our blind devotion to self or that which we idealize, we can see no reason worthy of doing so in the face of a threat to something we value highly. That is, we can find nothing more important than what we have already found to be important — no loyalties more compelling than those already sworn allegiance to and nothing more perfect or ideal than that already discovered.

This may be likened to our not learning to speak another language as long as the one we are using is adequate. When we wish or need to communicate with someone who doesn't speak our language, if no other recourse is available, we may trouble ourselves to learn something new. Precisely because it would be some trouble to learn the new language, we would look for other alternatives first. If we could not find one we might then endure the frustration of learning in order to communicate directly with someone different, someone new. Still, we must be highly motivated to do so. So it is with learning to think differently. Since it is frustrating to learn to think differently, we must be highly motivated in order to do it.

Despair As Motivation

What then might possibly motivate us to desire the containment of our desires at all, let alone to the point of pain or death? We are unlikely even to wish to become motivated to contain our desires as long as we find our present state offering the hope of attaining our desired state. As long as we can find a hope either in the self alone or in some other of attaining our desires, we will not

45

seek to transform our desires. Instead we will look to fine tune and perfect the existing mechanism. As long as we can hope in self, other, or some group movement or ideology, we will not seek true transformation of desire itself. We will only look beyond what we presently see, think beyond the way we now think, and feel beyond how we now feel, when we conclude that satisfaction by way of these familiar means is hopeless. We very much resist this conclusion and are adept at avoiding it. It might cause despair that is too disturbing to tolerate.

It does lead to despair but without despair many will never be motivated to seek the transformation of desire. We who will not be transformed by way of other means must tolerate despair for some period of crisis without resorting to numbing it or to destroying ourselves or some perceived frustrator in order to be motivated to change. This is the point at which all twelve step programs designed to deal with addictions introduce the idea that the self as a self alone is helpless to help itself, thus making the need to turn over the self to a Higher Power. This is the step we most resist. This turning over may be viewed as a submitting to, a holding of the values of the Higher Power at the center of the self, or a taking of the being or spirit of the Higher Power into the core of the self.

I have found it interesting that in discussions among mental health professionals when this step of the admission of the limits of self is introduced along with the idea of turning oneself over to a Higher Power, some therapists want to develop an alternative treatment without this step. The essence of the entire treatment is in this step. William James gives numerous personal accounts of this transformation of worldview that he terms "regeneration" in his classic writing *The Varieties Of Religious Experience*. This is the step in which we find the greatest offense. The recognition of human limits that apply to all humans by virtue of being human is repugnant to the autonomous, inflated self with its narcissism, its sense of entitlement, and its grandiosity. The self-centered person finds this turning over of the self to be foolishness. The egoistic self feels that it should not give up its egoism and refuses to consider doing so. Perhaps by definition of being autonomous, this self is unable to consider the possibility of giving the self over to a Higher Power.

Nevertheless, the ambivalent divided self cannot escape its ambivalence by itself. It can only become unambivalent when it sees one action or a decision in one direction as more important than another. This is what we do most of the time about small matters. We remain unambivalent by minimizing the consequences of most actions. If a decision has major consequences we are almost always ambivalent, for we have no way of truly knowing in advance what will satisfy our desires most for the longest period of time.

The only way I can subordinate my own desires is to have a devotion to and a willingness to serve something or someone that I determine to be more important than myself. In the context of this other whom I serve, be it a master, a Higher Power, or even only a principle by which I make choices if I am actually willing to live and die for it, I can then accept which of my desires must be subordinated to which others if it is necessary to do so. In the service to this higher or more idealized other I can reorder my desires in accord with its desires. This is why the "power" in Alcoholics Anonymous and other twelve-step type programs must be a *Higher* Power. It must be more important than we as individuals are. Otherwise we would not agree to serve it and make its desires, as we best understand them, more important than our own.

We will, in fact, idealize something, so should it not be something worthy of idealization? Should it not be something that can be perfect? Should it not be a Higher Power? Should we not reserve idealization for something beyond ordinary human endeavors no matter how good the cause? Is a political party, a charity, or any social movement worthy of idealization to the point of seeing it as perfect?

Serving any of these causes wholeheartedly will give at least some organizing principle to the self, but could we believe in their value to the point of giving up other pleasures, let alone life itself, in their service? Will the self really accept the subordination of its desires, that is the death of the self as it has been known thus far,

47

for anything other than a power or a being that is above us as humans? We risk our lives much less readily for other causes. When soldiers are sent into battle, usually the fight is somehow made to be for God as well as for country.

To sacrifice the self for another being requires a love that is greater than the love of self. This, of course, is not easy to come by. However, the willingness to love something outside of the self more than we love ourselves enables the inner ordering and organization of the self in a most adaptive way. This is true because it assists in establishing priorities. In part the love or zeal for the heroic may prompt self-sacrifice, but the attachment to the other that compels the sacrifice or risk of self-sacrifice seems a more primary component because it is the attachment to the other that compels living in service to it moment-to-moment on an ongoing basis.

Becker has suggested that we can enter into an "*agape* merger" with another or a group that will provide the context and meaning for our actions if we give the self over to the other. He finds this to be akin to the motive of "Christian love." Yet he proposes this without a Higher Power of any sort in the scheme of things. The assertion that this type of *agape* merger as some equivalent to "Christian love" can occur without at least a Higher Power, if not a Higher Power valuing self-sacrifice, seems unlikely if we are to hope for those using the defense of an inflated or autonomous sense of self to join in. Such people with their narcissistic traits, including treating others as objects, are in all likelihood not about to sacrifice themselves for just another poor old human being or even a group of human beings. Narcissistically self-centered, autonomous individuals regard others at the very best no more highly than themselves. Given that the choice is between human beings, the egocentric, autonomous-minded one would probably choose himself or herself. Were they capable of the sacrifice of their life, or any major sacrifice for another, they would not be who they are. One who is an autonomous self in the extreme, grandiose or narcissistic, or one with significant traits like this will often sacrifice the self only for a Higher Power or a God who must be served because of a recognized need for this God. Once this dependence is recognized and accepted, self-centeredness decreases. Though an overly autonomous self might serve another, lesser master, insofar as a dependency on this master was recognized, the autonomous self resists the recognition of and the state of dependence on another for the very reason that the self can then be compromised. The self-centered individual will resist the state of dependence on anything or anyone as long as possible. Only when the autonomous self is seen to be dependent on a Higher Other by being unable to master itself completely by itself will there be a submission of the self to the Higher Other.

An autonomous self trapped in conflicting desires may, in the collapse of the self-centered self, make a move to live for the Higher Other of *agape* love. The self-centeredness is changed and the person is now able to live in *agape* love with others not only because he must obey that which the self is now organized around (the Higher Power) but also because this Higher Power is loved and identified with. The self has been preserved in part but only by way of identification with the God of *agape* love who now not only must be served but who is lovingly and willingly served to prevent the self from collapse in its own conflicting desires and fears. This appears to be part of what is meant by the dying "unto the self" and being "born anew" or "born from above" in Christianity.

The deity depicted in many religions is one who demands sacrifices be made to it. The God of Jesus is a deity who is to have emptied himself into human form in order to make a sacrifice of himself on behalf of humanity. This is the model of self-sacrifice: a giving out of love when such giving was not forced or coerced. Unless we take such a God of self-sacrifice as the center of ourselves we are trapped in the idealization of something less, something that either has no hope of being perfect, all powerful, or everlasting, or is less of a model of self-sacrifice.

If the solution to despair and existential angst is so clear, why do we resist it? As in psychotherapy, hope might be offered if one would make a major change in the approach to life. Once it is discovered that this change is radical or major, many begin resisting the treatment. Change was fine as long as it would be not too much, in the right places, and most importantly, under the control of the self. The notion that the basic self must change is frightening since we then feel "I" will die.

Once I had worked for a long time with a person. We were getting to the point where I was going to make some key comments about his core personality traits. Understanding this, he lay back in the chair, closed his eyes, and said, "Okay, Doc, amputate." While this exaggerates what is possible, it is a good example of how it feels to consider, let alone actually make, major changes in the self, regardless of the cause or the means. We feel as if all or part of our self will die. We fear the cessation of a part of our being. Particularly we fear the loss of self-determination, choice, and self-control. Even if it is that very aspect of our being that has us in a knot, we at least feel more comfortable with the illusion of "freedom" of the will or the ability to choose.

If we are to put something at the center of our being other than our own "will," especially an all-powerful God, then the change is all the more frightening. At least in psychotherapy one will leave the therapist in the office and the therapist's powers are certainly limited. God, however, could follow us anywhere and everywhere. We are right to intuit that to allow such a God into the center of the self is to give over the entire self to that God. It means we must give over both emotional clusters, the cluster of feelings associated with pleasure and attachment in addition to the cluster associated with pain and destruction. Thus, both our pursuit of happiness and our avoidance of pain, our attachments and our aggression, must be included in that which we have given over to this God in order for them to be under the control of *agape* love. Lay aside for the moment, if you will, the particulars of how such control might be exercised and how the Being of this God would come to the center of the self until the concern of our resistance to it has been discussed.

Trusting That "God Is Great *And* God Is Good"

For the most part, we might think ourselves ready to give over the pain and aggression to the God of *agape* love to contain, but we do not like the giving over of our pursuit of pleasure and happiness. In fact, it seems that there are many who attempt the partial move of giving over to God their despair, anxieties, and sense of pain without giving over either their potential or actual anger and aggression or their pursuit of pleasure and their desires. So we attempt to cling to control of not only the positive emotional state but also the possible use of anger and aggression for the protection of the positive cluster of emotions. We believe that we must, in order to protect ourselves from evil (destruction), retain our own tools of evil (anger and aggression).

We do not wish to give over control or self-determination of the pursuit of happiness, at least in part because we will not trust this all-powerful God to be all-loving and benevolent. We would doubt the goodness of God even if we were to believe God exists. We doubt that God will not allow that which is truly bad for us. We don't trust this God even if we acknowledge that God is or may be real. There are some understandable reasons why we don't trust the goodness of God and understandable reasons why we wish to retain a sense of self-determination concerning our anger and aggression.

Among the many possible reasons, the most common include variations of these three:

1. We might transfer a sense of distrust or feelings of anger we have learned in relationships with others on whom we were dependent onto our image of God.

2. We might conclude that the reality of what the world, others, or God offer is lacking by comparison to what those on whom we were dependent as children provided.

3. Although it may be a modification of the last reason, we might find it impossible to believe in an all-powerful, all-loving God as long as evil exists in the world.

With each of these possibilities we attribute aspects of our own negative feeling cluster to God and in turn direct a part of the negative feeling cluster toward God. Then the God who is to be perfect, all-loving, and all-powerful, by way of our transferring emotions from other experiences or from a part of ourselves, comes to be seen by us as withholding, or angry, or impotent, or perhaps not there at all. These thoughts and feelings are much of the substance of doubt and resistance that would impede the giving over of the

51

self to God. In order to overcome doubt and resistance the sense of anxiety and despair of the egoistic self must be great since there can be no successful partial giving over of the self to God.

The Central Motive

There can be no partial giving over of the self because only one motive can occupy the centermost part of the self as primary. It is that center to which the rest of the self yields. To the degree that there is no such central motive or organizing center, the self is ineffectual because it is pulled in many divergent directions to act in different ways, all at the same time. Whatever the central motive is, it must be pre-imminent above all others and thus have reign over the entire self. This is true whether the central motive is the pursuit of the desires of the self, the pursuit of mutual idealization in romance, the pursuit of heroic service to the group, nation, and so on, or the pursuit of service to the God of *agape* love.

We do not trust God's goodness to a great extent because of all of the pain, suffering, death, and disease we see in the world. We demand reasons as to why such a God would permit these things to occur. And in essence we demand that God meet us on our terms, or we will refuse to believe that this God exists. If bad things occur, God must be unable to do anything about it, as Rabbi Kushner says in *When Bad Things Happen To Good People*. At that point God is not a real God by almost anyone's definition. If God can do nothing about such tragic and painful things, then many would not bother with God. An impotent God will not stand as a real God for most of us.

It seems that we will no longer consider that this God may be permitting things that cause us pain and that these events are not necessarily bad or evil. We won't consider this because our human-centered rationality insists that *we* must understand or be given access to why this would be. But we also will not or cannot differentiate within our negative emotional cluster that which is painful from that which is bad. If it hurts us it seems that we feel it is bad, wrong, or evil. If it causes us pain we usually will not consider that it might somehow be neutral if not good in some way we don't see.

52

This shows that our reasoning is greatly determined by our emotions. Whether there is any greater good to come of our pain, too often, is of no concern to us. We'd just rather not have the pain.

When I was in college, a girlfriend broke up with me and I was distraught. A professor told me that I'd be stronger because of the experience. I replied that I didn't want to be stronger, I just wanted to be happy. This is how we are for the most part. Our wishes to be happy or have our desires gratified are so god-like in importance that we will not consider as a possible reality a God who would allow us to hurt for some purpose. When we hurt because of a loss due to something which is beyond human control, we may feel a generalized bitterness or anger towards the cosmos, chance, fate, or whatever. This resentment can prevent belief in the God of *agape* love. If we believe in God then we may feel we should not be angry with God even if we are. If these feelings of anger from the negative emotional cluster remain uncontained by feelings from the positive emotional cluster, they may adversely affect our image of God.

The failure to deal with our anger toward God for permitting that which we feel is bad leaves us with two split-off God images, one for each cluster of feelings. We have the sense of love and attachment and thankfulness for all that we can consider to be good as we see it. We also have our feelings of resentment for all that we feel is bad and painful directed, if not to God, then to something perhaps outside of our awareness. Unacknowledged feelings of anger due to this can "leak" out toward anyone at any time and result in an act of violence. Keeping the negative emotional cluster under tight wraps may increase evil rather than bury it. As long as we retain those split-off images of God we are like the infant who does not realize that it is one and the same caretaker who withholds at one time and who at another time gratifies. We do not integrate our own feelings of goodness and badness concerning ourselves in early childhood until we master them first with our caretaker. I would say that this integration and mastery of feelings must be done again with God. This task in relation to God, when completed, allows us to consider that what God permits that causes us pain may not necessarily be bad and may work for our overall betterment in some way. Yet it is the sense that all of the badness we see must mean there is no all-loving God, that may keep us from this God.

God As A Magnet

Admittedly, there is a great divide, a chasm, between the state of our condition in doubt and ambivalence, with all of the defenses in place to keep things as they are within us and the state of belief in the God of *agape* love and a sense of completeness. Fear and pain from the negative emotional cluster may prod us across a bridge and into belief. A sense of attachment and oneness or feelings of goodness, thankfulness, and reverent awe may lure us across the chasm and into belief.

The bridging of the chasm, as it appears to me, involves the rupturing, leaking, or overflowing of one of the clusters of emotion which then floods the rest of the psyche. The experience may begin with one cluster and then the other following so that extremely intense and fluctuating emotions are felt. In this state of intense euphoria, oneness with the surrounding elements, heightened sensation with colors, for example, appearing brighter, feelings of peace and serenity, a reverence for nature, and an openness to others are likely to exist. Alternatively, there may be feelings of intense anxiety, despair, a sense of evil in the self and/or another, thoughts of death and destruction with the temptation to act on them, a sense of isolation and alienation from others, and dread, panic, or terror. Such a description is consistent with the individual cases presented by William James. They also match my own experience of descriptions I have heard from others, both in and out of the psychotherapeutic setting.

Such experiences are more likely to occur when the usual means of defending against and managing anxieties about living and dying have been stretched to the point at which they are felt, thought, or intuited to be inadequate. It is sensed that a new model of human existence and the world is essential in order to continue. An experience happens or a situation comes to the forefront that cannot fit into any of the categories of experience heretofore employed. That which has rested in the background has now shifted, it seems, to the foreground and it demands being attended to because now it will not be silenced.

The eruption may occur in response to one event or after years of searching. The searching might be for that which is perfect or most beautiful — a work of art, justice, physical beauty, or the perfect romance. If so, it is the pull of the desire within us to find something so perfect that it is Holy. We do not find our peace, then, until we experience that which we serve to be Holy. On the other hand, it may be after years of searching to escape a sense of anxiety, despair, death, destruction, or evil that we are prodded to seek its counterbalance in that which we sense to be Divine or Sacred. The experience may follow the search for the satisfaction of desire for most of a lifetime, only to be confronted with the futility of the search. It may follow decades of attempts to escape pain or suffering only to find that more always follows.

Augustine said that we are born with the image of this God within us and that we find no rest until we rest in God. These parts of the self and conditions may be within us, but it is also said that it is God himself that is the magnet that pulls on them, God himself who uses or permits the episodes of fear and terror to accomplish his purposes, God himself who holds the mirror up to the squanderer of life to haunt with the reflection, and God himself that lures us to fall into nothing short of a love that is desirous of this God of *agape* love. If oneness with this God of *agape* love is our primary desire, all other desires and fears can be contained within it and our desires are thereby transformed as are we ourselves. Even those of us who have been most self-centered are tamed by such a transforming.

Chapter 4

Acute Terror And Panic

Panic Attacks

It does not seem surprising to me at all that as a 26-year-old male graduate student my prelude to a sense of acute terror began with an internal conflict concerning a young woman. Everything in my brain was telling me that I'd be completely foolish to lose her since she was so attractive, good-hearted, and bright. Yet somehow in my stomach it didn't feel that we should develop a more serious relationship. I could not make sense of this apprehension since there were no apparent "good reasons" for it. I had always tried to run my life by good reasons, sound, logical, sober calculations that I thought would reveal the choice most advantageous to me. This dilemma had me terribly conflicted because I feared I would make a bad decision that would leave me deprived of something wonderful — the woman or my freedom. I didn't know which was most important to me, but a decision had to be made.

It felt as if the stakes were supremely high and that I had no means by which to know what to do. I wanted an answer that was guaranteed to be right. Part of me was in conflict with the rest of me, so I had no consistent sense of what to do. I shouldn't be uncomfortable physically, it seemed, with what my mind said I should do. Yet I was. It was one of those so very ordinary situations when at times the mind said to do one thing and at other times to do the opposite. This ordinary quandary was the beginning of some most unordinary experiences.

I lost my appetite and was unable to eat due to nausea. I slept poorly and some nights not at all because of the anxiety. After several days of this I was emotionally, mentally, and physically exhausted. Still, I was agitated and restless.

Then one evening, alone in my apartment, I began to have heart palpitations. It felt as if I would have a heart attack, the pounding was so strong. Having studied "anxiety attacks," I thought this might

57

be one but, "What if I might actually have a heart attack and die?" I worried. In the anxiety I eventually felt as if I had to look for help outside of myself to stop this. I didn't want to but I had tried to stop my heart from pounding and I couldn't. I had contained this tension too long.

I consulted a psychiatrist at the student health center and tried some medication. It didn't help. The heart palpitations and anxiety were as strong as ever when they came. I knew my anxiety was the product of attempting to avoid a decision that eventually had to be made. The heart palpitations didn't stop until I told myself that I would go ahead and die with the heart attack rather than be controlled by the palpitations. Although this seemed like a heroic act at the time, the anxiety simply returned in the form of the rapid flight of ideas and thoughts racing through my mind. I feared that I would go insane. This is a typical symptom of what today could be diagnosed as a "panic attack." Not knowing this, my panic increased.

I decided to let my mind and myself go with the hunches and my intuition wherever my imagination might lead me rather than try to suppress the thoughts. I wasn't sure I really could suppress them completely anyway. While my mind seemed to keep saying that my thoughts of terror were in my imagination, my emotions reacted as if what I feared was really happening. I felt tremendous anxiety and tension in my body. A tingling, crawling sensation in my thigh muscles and a gnawing emptiness in my stomach would come and go. Each time it came I felt as if it would never leave. It came to mind that if I would run and jump through the window and let my body smash on the pavement below then at least all of this physical discomfort would end. Then I thought this to be an awful, even an evil, idea, but I feared that I would feel compelled to do it.

A Profound Change

Sensing no inner resource capable of the task of letting me feel contained in some way from an act that I didn't want to do, I found myself in prayer to whatever Higher Power or God that might be there. "Just keep me from harming myself and let me remain sane,"

58

I muttered, although I was wondering just how sane I was at that moment. I wanted to be saved from myself.

I began to feel that a man staying near me whom I would see several times a day was, for reasons I could not discern, somehow evil. There seemed something demonic about him. The anxiety associated with this was so great that all I could do to keep the terror away was to repeat the Lord's Prayer over and over. I tried prayer after many attempts at self-reassurance that this was all in my imagination and many attempts at relaxation exercises. I always thought in part of my mind that the ideas I was experiencing were at least a bit bizarre. Nevertheless, I felt committed to follow them as long as they remained simply ideas, because I thought that somewhere through the maze there would be a way out. Given what followed in my thoughts I conclude that I was attributing an evil to this man that I sensed was in me. I believe I was sensing my destructive potential, which, in fact, we all have more of a capacity for than most of us feel comfortable acknowledging.

Soon I began to intuit that there was something that I can only call evil in me that had to come out. The story of Jesus healing a man possessed by demons came to mind. It probably came to mind because had I believed in demons, which I did not, I imagine that being possessed by them would have made me feel as I was feeling. I suspended my critical, rational self and asked myself, "What does it seem that I need to do to manage these feelings?" The thought arose within me that I must call upon God to remove from me whatever there was that was evil or demonic if such were there.

As I look back on this now, it seems to follow the therapeutic rule of responding to a patient's expressed fear by asking what it would mean to the patient if that which is feared were true; that is, to take the fantasy as if it were a reality and follow it rather than to dismiss it as irrational. All the while this was occurring I did not believe demons existed or that God, whatever he/she/it was, did anything much with human beings. My image of God was something akin to the impersonal "Force" from the *Star Wars* movies. Still, I followed the intuition. I felt as if I should open my mouth and imagine the demons leaving me and running out of the window just as I had imagined doing and crashing to death on the pavement below. Then the idea followed that Jesus was supposed to have cast demons into a herd of swine that then ran off a cliff, presumably to their destruction. For no reason 1 can think of, I sensed I should cross my feet and open my mouth during this. Seeing no harm in it I followed the inner sense of what I should do though I knew that it must have looked strange.

After this little exercise I was not bothered by these tormenting thoughts and feelings. I felt a great relief and began to come out of my turmoil. I realized that human consciousness has its limits with regard to what it can control and that at times it is unable to control the body it lives in, the emotions, and even what we think of as our own thoughts. I concluded that ordinarily we exaggerate in our own beliefs the degree of conscious control we have over our lives in general and over ourselves especially. This exaggerated sense of personal control is built on the massive denial of our true and profound limits. It is my sense that the emotional experience of these limitations may prompt one to debilitating anxiety that can result in self-destruction if something larger outside of the self and outside of the human domain is not sought as a container for the self. I felt dependent now on this God that I had sought as my container. I had to acknowledge my need of this God. Prior to this time acknowledging dependency on anything or anyone would've seemed repugnant to me, since, if I was dependent on it, I might be controlled by it. I have come to think that this is why many avoid God, given that otherwise acknowledging God may seem understandable and necessary to tolerate the anxieties of existence.

It came to mind that if I would reach for God in desperation then I could no longer kid myself as to my belief in this God as a Being that I could be in relation with. I felt that I must deepen my relatedness with that God even when not in a state of desperation. The conclusion that I could not ignore the God I had come to, prompted me to daily contemplative prayer.

Following the resolution of this crisis I experienced many times of elation, feeling in synchrony with all that was around me, and that I had finally coalesced as a solid "I" for the first time. I felt settled within myself and comfortable with myself. The colors of the grass, trees, and things of nature seemed brighter in hue and more intense than I had ever noticed. I wondered if this new-found self would be transitory.

One day I had the thought that God might be laughing at me and at all of us, not in a cynical way but chuckling at us for taking ourselves so very seriously. I came to suspect that God wanted us to join him in this gentle laughter at ourselves.

I decided to address whatever the psychological vulnerabilities were that had allowed me to become so emotionally distraught. I began psychoanalytically-oriented psychotherapy, which continued twice a week for two years. I became aware of much that I was not consciously aware of before, particularly by way of the examination of the thoughts and feelings I would have about the therapist (the transference).

I never felt that looking at my psyche from a psychological perspective was in any way problematic in relation to an experience that was both psychological and spiritual with regard to the outcome. Understanding my thoughts and feelings through psychotherapy was most helpful and enlightening. I assumed that many of my thoughts during the experience of panic were speculative, intuitive, and at points fantasy. However, the belief that there was definitely some type of God around, that I felt connected to it during prayer, and that this relating to God was critical in overcoming my fears of living, of dying, and of assuming responsibility for major decisions, was not at all fantasy. Thus, none of these matters were to be the focus of psychological treatment. It seemed undeniable to me that the product of this experience of crisis as a whole was beneficial and constructive. I functioned better and felt better after having gone through it. I would periodically now have a sense of "oneness" with other people and the world in general that I had never experienced before. Periods of serene ecstasy also came from time to time along with the abiding sense that somehow whatever happened would be all right. The moments of anxiety tapered off so that after a few weeks they were gone.

I was left at the end with a proper humility as I see it with regard to my ability and capacity to plan out all the particulars and control all the events in my life. My sense is that most of us walk around falsely buoyed up by an exaggerated estimation of our abilities to control the specific occurrences in our lives. A sense of inner balance has been with me ever since this time over 25 years ago. I have been much less likely to become angry or irritable and I have felt more compassionate towards others. A feeling that I am a part of what they are a part of has stayed with me. The craftsmanship of God has seemed apparent to me in human events as well as in nature. This alteration in my personality was perhaps more inwardly than outwardly apparent although it was obvious to many. The change left me prepared to live as well as possible with two trying events yet to come.

Making Sense Of Panic

Although I have said that my experience might accurately be diagnosed today as a panic attack, to me, this is not the key to understanding it. Perhaps a panic attack occurs when certain existential realities common to all humans crash through the normal defenses that ordinarily enable us either to tune these realities out, minimize them, or intellectualize them. Perhaps in certain situations or at certain times we are all vulnerable to a hyper-awareness of our extreme fragility on this earth. Perhaps at times we may become hyper-aware either at an intuitive level or a conscious level of the limits of our human life, such as our limited duration of life, that we cannot have everything we want, and that this is so in part because we cannot decide even within ourselves on what we really want most. In short, as Paul Tillich has written in *The Courage To Be*, we are anxious about our dying and the fear that we will then not exist at all, though that may not be a conscious fear. We are anxious about our living and what the consequences of our decisions in life will be and what our fate in life will be. We are afraid that our lives will be meaningless or less than what they might be. When these realities close in on us and we see the limited amount of influence we have on the outcome of so many matters of importance in life, it is frightening.

My panic was the result of the acute and sudden awareness of these realities. I was unable to deny emotionally the awesomeness of the major dilemmas of human life that we ordinarily tune out since thinking about them is too disruptive of the necessary focusing on day-to-day survival. Feelings about my vulnerability and puniness in the face of death broke through into a heightened conscious awareness, as did anxiety with the emotional recognition that my life — all of our lives — could be permanently altered for the worse by the making of a particular decision. Painfully, we have no way to gain the foresight to enable us to truly "know" what the best decision is. I realized how fragile our "rationality" is and how emotions associated with wishes and fears can be so powerful as to leave this wonderful rationality in a position where it is divided against itself. I was now aware that my emotions, too, could be terribly divided and conflicting. The self then could not trust itself alone to rescue itself because it could not reconcile its conflicting parts without the loss of something or the giving up of something. And the self of the self-centered person is very set against giving something up.

In the determined pursuit not to give up anything, the state of conflict can be heightened to the point of a crisis that demands a new self view and a new world view to resolve the crisis successfully. This new world view, I concluded, puts the self as secondary to God. Something outside of this divided self was needed to help it resolve the impasse, but it was the self that would have to reach for it.

Further, it seemed that this sense of evil was too overwhelming to contain myself since it produced such a great fear. In all likelihood the sense of evil was itself the product of the fear of some type of annihilation. It was almost as if the self-centered aspect of myself could fear that it was to be reigned in and wanted me to feel as if my entire being would be destroyed if it were restrained. The fear of this evil promoted a desire for its opposite — the Holy, the Sacred, or the Perfect — in order to contain it.

I see the potential for the emotional experience of both that which seems evil and that which seems sacred to be within each of us. The daily preoccupations of life prevent or distract us from focusing on such matters most of the time. Occasionally in sleep, in a state of fatigue, or in crisis when the defenses are down, we experience something akin to what the Danish theologian Soren

Kirkegaard, who experienced it most of his life, called the sense of "dread." It can break through and overwhelm the psyche.

At this point of dread, panic, or terror we see the human condition quite differently. We notice more the apparently pathetic, futile, tragic, destructive, or hopeless aspects of human beings. In a sense we then realize with our emotions the seeming despair, nihilism, and acute tension of existentialist writers such as Camus. This is what I felt in the state of terror or panic. I felt that I had to look outside of the despairing, terrorized self to find an adequate container for this "it" which was me.

This means of change was not willingly chosen by me since I would never have intentionally agreed to the experience of panic. But, as egoistic as I was, I doubt that any other means of change could have worked so effectively. The sense of terror and panic pulled from me the prop of pride and arrogance on which my sense of self had rested.

Chapter 5

Paralysis

A Stunning Moment

After working as a psychologist for a year and a half, five months shy of being thirty, I was exercising one night with light barbells as usual. I lay down on my bed to rest for a few minutes. When I tried to get up, my left arm and leg wouldn't move. I was shocked. I tried again and again, not knowing what to make of this since there was neither any obvious injury nor any pain. Then I threw myself out of my bed attempting to force my body to work, but as I fell to the floor only my right arm and leg flew out to break the fall. I pounded on the floor so that friends below in the kitchen would hear me. I yelled for them to call the rescue squad.

I had no idea what was happening. The only warnings had been fleeting muscle weakness several times in my neck and knee that occurred after weight-lifting. I'd assumed it was muscle fatigue. Perhaps this was a form of hysterical paralysis, I thought, being unaware of any other cause. There was no warning. I never lost consciousness and there was no pain.

The ambulance came. I was carried from my room on a stretcher to the ambulance where I was given oxygen. My left leg was shaking and trembling uncontrollably. I began to pray the Lord's Prayer slowly and repeatedly as I had during the episodes of panic in graduate school. I was calmed.

As the ambulance drove into the hospital we passed under the huge neon sign reading "Emergency Room." Instantly I recalled that as a theology student seven years earlier I had walked by that sign daily on the way to my apartment and felt it had some meaning for me, as if it were foretelling something bad to come my way. The foreboding was strong enough that when I moved away I felt a relief and thought, "Well, nothing's going to happen to me in connection with this sign. After all, I've escaped it." But when I returned to the city and walked past it the first time I thought, "Oh, no, now I've got to live under this sign again." Riding under this

65

sign in the ambulance it felt as if what had been feared was now occurring. I make nothing particular of what seems a "premonition" of sorts and don't see it as significant. It does prompt me to have a sense either that some things may be foreordained or that we somehow may intuit beforehand what indeed does happen. I'm not one who has such premonition-like thoughts frequently. They've come to me a very few times in my life and when they have, it has seemed relevant to the events that unfolded. The primary matter appears to be that the events occur and we respond to them in a particular way.

Upon arrival at the hospital emergency room, I gave all the insurance and personal information myself at the registration desk. I was awake the entire night with tests, including brain scans. Eventually, I was told that I had had a "cerebrovascular accident" due to an "arteriovenal malformation that was probably congenital." In short, one of the blood vessels in my brain had leaked due to its being malformed from birth. It, in all likelihood, was going to leak sooner or later and it had done so now. Surgery was advised to remove the vessel so that it wouldn't leak again. The surgery was serious and entailed a small (probably less than two percent) chance of death, the risk of worse damage to more than just the "motor area" of the brain affecting physical movement, and a small chance of blindness or partial blindness. However, I was told that without the surgery there was a twenty percent chance of bleeding again, which might result in worse paralysis or death. I weighed the alternatives with the neurosurgeon and agreed that surgery was the thing to do. Going through whatever of life was left with what would feel like a "time bomb" in my head would cause more anxiety due to the uncertainty and a game of higher stakes throughout the rest of life than I'd live well with. Settling the ambiguity now — life or death, and if life, under what conditions — felt best to me.

The night before the surgery my left leg, no longer under voluntary control, had a frequent tremor. I slept very little at all. Somewhere around 5 a.m. a nurse came to me and asked if she could do anything for me before surgery. I asked her to read the Twenty-third Psalm. Then I felt ready for the surgery. Though I did feel prepared for my life to end if that were to happen (and I told my parents this in case the surgery wasn't successful), I felt hopeful that I'd make it in some condition. I recall having had something beyond a thought of "What if I have to die soon?" a few weeks before all of this occurred. My answer to myself took the form of the thought that I did not feel ready for my consciousness, memories, and experiences of life to end, and I prayed that my life would not end soon. I also had the thought about that time that my growth in closeness to God had not increased recently and that I would do and accept what was necessary to increase my relatedness to God. I am giving here an account of my experience. I don't conclude that what happened to me was necessarily in response to this nor do I feel convinced that God directly caused this or anything else that has happened to me personally. However, I do not rule that possibility out either. It seems egoistic or grandiose to say that I am sure these or other occurrences in my life were intentionally caused by God. Perhaps they were, but I also believe that they may have occurred by whatever random chance God permits in this world. To me the important matter is what we do with what happens to us and how we do it.

The surgery went well although I could tell that others were frightened by the appearance of my head, misshapen by swelling after surgery. It was a humbling experience to see others frightened by my appearance. It was as if the sight of me made them realize acutely that something devastating to the body had happened to me and, in fact, could happen to anyone, themselves included. To be seen as pitiable and to know that it is true forces a certain seeing of the self — at least the body — as a thing. Such a "seeing" can prompt the sense of the self as separate or dissociated somewhat from the body and whatever the body does. Likewise, in keeping with the common tendency after such damage, I found, for example, my left hand could be forgotten on the table next to my cereal bowl until I'd turn around only to find that the left hand had spilled the cereal on the floor when I had turned. Having lost muscular control of my left side I was unable to trigger bowel and bladder functions and needed assistance, including catheterization. There was only half of "me" that I was in control of; the other half felt like a lifeless side of meat.

One night I found it hard to breathe. It felt as if my left lung wasn't going to continue working. Not being able to get my breath aroused fear again. The physician came. The lung muscle was weak but functioning. It was a false but frightening alarm.

A Long And Steep Climb

A few days after the surgery, I was taken to a nearby rehabilitation center where I would stay and receive therapy for my arm and leg each twice a day. I was confined to a wheelchair when not in bed. Life for the novice in a wheelchair also forces a reckoning with pride since I had to ask for help opening the door and assistance with many of the normal activities of daily living. A young man from the rescue squad who had been with the crew that came for me visited me. He sat quietly except to comment that he was struck by the degree of serenity I'd had during the ambulance ride. I had not been aware of feeling at all serene and was surprised by the comment. I thought then that any composure I did have in response to my physical trauma was the result of my encounter with panic and terror in graduate school. At the rehabilitation center I was encouraged by the visit of at least one person from my church every day for the entire three months I was an inpatient.

Life at the rehabilitation center was a protected experience in that visits to the real world outside were not frequent. When I was taken out, I was struck again by people staring at me, whereas back at the center everyone else was handicapped too.

Oddly, it seemed the day for discharge from the rehabilitation center came too soon because I wasn't back to normal yet. Knowing that other parts of the brain could assume the functions formerly done by the now-damaged area, I had hoped to be fully recovered when I was discharged. I had been elated the day I first moved a finger. I had hoped it would all return just as the finger did. I'd also been elated with leg movement, standing and then walking with a cane even though I had a substantial limp and could not lift my left foot off the floor still or move quickly at all. I'd hoped to be much better than I was, if not fully recovered, by discharge time. So I was disappointed in part about how far I'd come. Perhaps things will still improve with time, I thought.

Leaving the protected inpatient world and returning home was difficult. What if I could never return to work? I spent the days at home alone apart from my daily trip in to the city for therapy Monday through Friday. The physical therapist told me I would probably never run again. I knew she was telling me gradually that I'd never fully recover. I managed to fall more than I had expected and this greatly worried others, especially when the fall was down a flight of stairs.

I had hoped to return to work right away. I felt that at least then some part of me would be back to normal. I learned that it was recommended that I not return to work for another three months while I continued therapy daily as an outpatient. I felt shattered.

An old friend came to visit me one day. As we talked, she put her arms around me. I don't recall exactly what she said but whatever it was it pushed the button and for the first time I cried. I wept. I wept for myself. I wept for what it seemed I would never get back completely. I wept for what had happened to me and for what I had lost.

I had flashes of anger at any predicament that called attention to my new limitations. The cat would get into something on the shelf and it seemed to know that I could no longer catch it, so the cat would "defy" me. Nemeses such as this one were the focus whenever I was angry which, oddly, was very rare. Yet I retained the feeling that despite all that had happened and however I would be, I would be in some sense all right. All of this, I thought, could have some good outcome. People I knew would see that this could happen to anyone. It would make others wonder how they'd feel and how they would manage if it happened to them. It would make people think of our vulnerability and mortality. This left me feeling no inclination to weep again for myself though I did sorely miss being able to dance and was anxious about my appearance with all of the residual spasticity in my left arm and leg. For whatever reason, I believed God was with me in this horrible situation. Without this belief I can only imagine that I would've felt desperate and at least chronically depressed. How I retained this belief that God was with me and that something "good enough" would come from all of this I cannot say. It seemed to come to me effort-lessly and thus I can claim no credit for it. I do believe that had I not come to God earlier, traversing this crisis would have been impossible to imagine.

Trying to date again was painful. The worries of risking rejec-tion from high school days returned but realizing now the striking reason why I'd be rejected — my crippled, handicapped body — hurt. It wasn't as bad as I'd anticipated, but at times I must've seemed pitiful to the women who'd go to dinner with me. I had someone over for dinner, forgetting that I'd be unable to scoop cold, hard ice cream from the box without the ice cream landing on the floor. It did. I acquired a familiarity with being stared at and being asked what had happened to me. My self-consciousness seemed a form of great torture. Seeing my limping, contorted body reflected in a large store window felt like a dentist's drill on my psyche. It was a form of torment for me since I always had been somewhat preoccupied with my appearance. I saw the movie *The Elephant Man* and identified with this deformed creature, for that is just what I felt like. I was greatly exaggerating the similarity between the elephant man and myself, I realize, but in my inner world we seemed much alike.

I felt a bit like the prince who had a spell cast over him, which turned him into a beast until a beauty would love him. I wondered who in her right mind would romantically love one as crippled as I was now. Perhaps I should look for someone else with a disability or handicap. Dating again was a major thing for me to contend with in part because I was sure that before this felt ruination of my body I would never have even dated a person with a disability. I was always looking for and generally found someone others and I thought was very attractive.

After six months I returned to work, talking more slowly and deliberately, walking less than half of normal speed, and with much awkwardness. I was nurtured by the good friendships with the people I worked with who had remained faithful visitors and sources of support throughout my absence.

Reflections On Paralysis

Several inner changes occurred following my paralysis. Increasingly I felt myself trying to make it less and less important to me how my body appeared and how it functioned or didn't function. This more-than-usual dissociation of the sense of self from the body that a disability or other physical trauma may produce seems to me both common and adaptive. I have heard of this dissociation of the sense of self and the body from others following major surgery for heart problems. It may be a similar kind of dissociation that to some degree the spiritually-focused person, according to many writings on spiritual development, is also required to do in order not to be overly identified with bodily existence. I noticed that whereas in the past I would have blamed problems on others or circumstances outside of myself, a capacity to sit still with the problem and accept some or most of the responsibility for it myself, when warranted, grew. Since I now felt far from perfect in many ways, I was more able to accept the lack of perfection and shortcomings of others. I am convinced that this helped in being able to remain married happily and keep working in the same position with enjoyment. Prior to my physical disability, my tendency was to "move on" when problems arose. Having been able to start again with some ease, I'd never developed the ability to accept another or a situation that I felt limited me in any way. I began to see my destructive, irritable, and arrogant tendencies being tamed. My tendency to avoid admitting to errors and changing aspects of myself by avoiding lasting commitments was now held in check by my recognition that it would not be easy to start again elsewhere. It now seemed that it would, in fact, be most difficult to move, adjust to a new place, and find new friends and a new job.

An increasing willingness to let go of self and be a "branch on the vine" resulted from and led to a greater inner harmony, which in turn led to a greater harmony with others. It seems unlikely to me that anything would have made me willing to let go of my self-interest or grasp it less, other than something that induced the fear that I, as the self, or a part of me, might be destroyed.

In my arrogance and self-centeredness I would not have willingly changed much. Only by having my "feet held to the fire" by

71

the destruction of parts of my identity and parts of my bodily functioning or something of this order would I be made malleable enough to change. I cannot deny that the changes have been toward the better. Likewise, I cannot deny that a part of me wishes they would have come about in a different way.

Believing that God is sovereign, and that if he is not then he is not God as most have thought of God, I must believe that God can directly cause and indirectly permit such things as tragedies to happen to us. This does not seem cruel to me if the result is good insofar as God in his singular wisdom would call it good. Only my grandiosity would lead me to insist that I must know why and how this is good, or whether it could have come about by other means. If for some reason God actually and directly causes a painful event to occur and the one experiencing the pain believes this to be so, then the pain as well as the entire event can take on a particular meaning. In such a case, the idea that God "elects" specific individuals to have particular experiences may be applicable. I have never held the notion that I was "elected" or chosen in some way for these experiences to happen to me. Yet I do not believe that anyone should completely reject such possibilities, as we cannot presume to know the mind of God. My discomfort with believing this with regard to myself goes beyond simply the wish to avoid being presumptuous in claiming to know the mind of God. Such a highly personalized explanation seems a bit too self-centered for me to feel comfortable with, while at the same time attempting to become increasingly less self-centered.

This sovereign God may also permit, rather than cause directly, such things to happen to us by way of doing nothing to prevent pain from coming our way. I choose to interpret what has happened to me more as permitted. In believing that God did not attempt to intervene with the processes of nature that he set into motion and could alter, I am left to feel that whatever it is that God has allowed to happen is just that — allowable. Thus, he did not deem that the normal processes of nature should be interrupted in order to spare me whatever pain came my way. If God will "allow" this physical damage to my body as tolerable, then perhaps I need also look at it as tolerable, I thought, and therefore not a matter of the greatest importance. Other matters must be at least somewhat more important to God. If nothing else, preventing the occurrence was not more important than circumventing nature's course. My response must then become one of "How can I do whatever is best with myself given what and who I am now?" I must continue to look at myself not as the center of the world but rather a being in God's world and seek how I might contribute the most and be of the greatest use for God's purposes as best I can understand them.

An important question with regard to believing painful occurrences are allowed by God and therefore must be accepted by humans can arise with regard to evil. Does this suggest then that the Holocaust was allowed by God and should therefore be acceptable to humans? I would assert that it does not. The Holocaust was caused by human beings with either evil intentions or disturbed thought processes or both. This seems different to me than tragedy caused by the elements of nature devoid of human intention or design. For God to have intervened to prevent the Holocaust it seems he would have had to tamper with the freedom of human wills. Nevertheless, we must be struck by the apparent fact that God has permitted and allowed murderous, psychotic thoughts to prompt evil acts by human beings — a part of his creation. Given that humans succumb to the temptation to kill even without a psychosis present, it seems that we have been created as all too vulnerable to temptation, especially the temptation of rage.

There is a beauty in the belief that God has some part in the process of what our fate in life is. This beauty, to me, is that I can ultimately hold only God "accountable" for permitting it especially if no humans brought the event about. Thus, any anger that I may have about my circumstances, I must address to God. This contains and binds resentment that might otherwise spill out toward other people. It is significant, as I see it, that any anger I might have is felt then towards God for whom I also feel much love.

Therefore, the feelings of anger may be bound and contained by this love. This is akin to the anger a child might feel towards a parent for imposing some limits on the child's behavior being neutralized by the love for the parent. If the process goes the other way, the love is overwhelmed by the rage. Perhaps the parent in such

73

instances is not acting in the child's best interest, but rather for self-centered reasons and the child sees this. The child is not trusting the parent's motives to be good. As an adult I believe that I must challenge myself to believe that God will not act in a sadistic manner toward me by allowing that which I cannot use well toward his purposes to happen to me if I remain in communion with him. If I find that I mistrust God's intentions then it seems that I must make every effort to correct that thought so that I see God as loving and do come to trust him. Undeniably, in this position is the belief, simply said, that whatever happens to us we can use constructively to advance God's general purposes with humankind.

This becomes a greater challenge if we believe that painful events even when caused by other malevolent persons can be used to advance that which is good. Does it not show a more wonderful love of God if we can love him in spite of what he has permitted to happen to us that causes pain or suffering? At that point we have transcended our self-centered selves and risen above the pain we have experienced so that we can consider that it might not be an "all bad" or "evil" occurrence. Perhaps there is some good in it by way of bringing someone into closer communion with God. What if it is by way of human agony that this is brought about? Of course, we don't like it. We don't like it, I imagine, because it hurts. Nevertheless, we must remember that it is the God of Christianity who elected that the Messiah, the Christ, should die a painful death by crucifixion. It is consistent with both the Old and the New Testaments that the Judaeo-Christian God permits and causes human suffering to fulfill his ends. Our God is a God who at times initiates pain, which leads to suffering. Our God in the scriptural record often uses destruction and suffering to bring about his intentions. Our God is a God that joins us in suffering by taking on our suffering as his own such as in coming into the world in human form and knowingly assuming suffering and pain. Perhaps suffering and pain due to both accident and evil seal our bond with this God and help us attach to him.

Romance

There was a woman whom I had noticed at a distance working at the rehabilitation center with elderly patients. Although I knew all of the other therapists well, I had carefully avoided meeting this therapist. I had the thought that if I ever went back to work and was feeling better about myself, I'd ask her to dinner, so I didn't want her to notice how I looked then. I was apprehensive about calling her and feared what she'd say to me and what she'd think of me for asking her to go to dinner with me. Finally, with prodding from a friend, I called and asked her. She agreed to go. On the way to the restaurant we had to walk a block after parking the car. I felt that I was walking more slowly than a snail though she said nothing about it and didn't appear bothered by my pace. Just before reaching the restaurant a man sitting on a wall by the sidewalk spoke loudly to me, "Hey, what happened to you?" I answered, showing no emotion, although I wanted to disappear.

The first date was punctuated at the end of the evening by her telling me a list of her faults as if I wouldn't want to call her again if I knew them. Perhaps, I speculated, she thought this would keep me away and that was her preference. I also learned that she was from Denmark and had been working in the United States for five years. She wasn't a citizen of this country and didn't intend to become one. At this first dinner we talked about what we imagined the future held for each of us and that at some time we each hoped to marry and have a family. I was very taken with her. Her quietness and introversion, balanced with poise, were intriguing. She had smiled and laughed it seemed continuously with her patients when I watched her at work. Now she was reflective, more serious. The next day I wondered if sending her flowers would show me to be too eager. I sent them anyway and a couple of days later she called and invited me over for dinner. I learned that she'd stayed up until 2 a.m. making Danish pastry for dessert. I guessed that I rated a bit with her then. She seemed not to notice what to me was a glaring disability.

We dated more, saw each other more frequently, and grew closer. I wondered why she'd get involved with me. Was it because she worked with the elderly handicapped and was so familiar with disability that it didn't stand out to her? Was it because she was from a culture where physical appearances meant less? I didn't know.

Finally, one evening I told her that I knew that her accepting me with a disability and deepening our relationship would cost her something since I wouldn't be able to do some things with her that she enjoyed, such as dance and hike. I told her that I'd manage to adjust, if she felt it was best, without her while I tried to refrain from showing my feelings of attachment to her. I wanted to know now if she was going to break off with me because of my disability, and I wanted her to consider carefully what was best for her.

She reacted with seriousness and it seemed she was, in fact, going to take this as an opportunity to back away from me. It felt good in an odd way to experience the fear of losing her. These emotions were familiar from college days, and I felt alive in a way I hadn't in many months. We left it that we should take a period of absence from each other and think about whether we wished to continue getting closer. I felt sick with agitation the next day. I thought I'd come across as too indifferent and that she'd conclude I didn't want to continue seeing her. After work I drove immediately to the rehabilitation center and waited for her to come out. I told her I cared for her very much and thought that I should have said that too, but hadn't the day before. I said that I didn't want to stop seeing her and that I was sure I wanted the relationship to continue but I'd felt that in fairness to her I had to give her this opportunity to leave me. It became very clear in those moments that she didn't want to leave me. Six months later on Valentine's Day I made what I thought of as an official proposal of marriage though we'd begun already to speak as if we'd have a future together. She invited me to go to Denmark with her that summer to meet her family. She wanted to wait until the following Christmas when we could both take time away from work to return to Denmark so that we could be married there. Our wedding was planned for two years to the day from my cerebral hemorrhage.

I felt some sense of victory that day in having not only lasted through two years of physical therapy and rehabilitation, but also to be back to work and marrying. We were married on the tiny island of Bornholm, Denmark, which is twenty miles on each of its four sides and located in the middle of the Baltic Sea.

The morning of our wedding at 6 a.m. her relatives began arriving at the house having sailed all night on a boat leaving from the Danish mainland. The tiny house was packed with relatives. An endless parade of breakfast rolls of many kinds were brought in. The coffee, tea, and schnapps flowed all morning. The ceremony was in a Danish Lutheran church that was several hundred years old and looked over the main harbor. Together with the equally old small houses surrounding the church, it gave the impression of a place one sees in paintings but that doesn't really exist. All but a very few of the wedding guests were relatives. Everyone appeared to have known everyone else very well and for years. The ceremony was marked throughout by a confident dignity.

After the wedding a bus took all of the guests to the reception at an inn in the woods. The toasts to the exclamation, "Skoal," continued as they had in the morning. A meal with multiple courses, each served twice by the servers, followed. In between courses, songs were sung to us. The words were written to familiar tunes by various groups of guests and were designed to tenderly tease us and wish us well. They were also a "farewell and good-bye" between the lines to my wife. They realized she'd now really be moving to the United States and not just working abroad for a while. The last of these songs, of which a copy was passed out to each guest, was wrapped around a candle. During the singing the candles were lit in the dim room and the guests came around us in two lines from opposite directions for each one to place the candle in a centerpiece before us. If eating from gold plates and utensils, as was the custom for the bride and groom at a wedding, hadn't made me feel we were receiving treatment reserved for the most important of people and occasions, this did. Mostly though, I felt completely accepted. There was a warm love that I could feel towards us and a communality with us engendered especially by this last song.

After a dessert and having a stomach that felt fuller than I could ever recall, the band, complete with accordion, played into the early morning hours. As always in Denmark, something else was eaten at the end though there had been chocolates and coffee after dessert. I had been worried that I wouldn't be able to do the required dance with the bride, my mother-in-law, and sister-in-law, yet I was able to do not only enough dancing, but also to enjoy it. I felt I had come a long way from my surgery bed two years earlier. The beauty and glow of this wedding and all the festivities were beyond what I could have imagined.

We came back to the United States and slowly acquired furniture for our home. We had our first child two years later. Experiencing her birth increased my reverence for life. Three years later we had a son who was to be with us for only a little over half a year.

Chapter 6

The Life And
Death Of A Son

A Difficult Birth

As I now recall you, little boy, seven years after losing you, I still have no adequate understanding of why our God, whom I believe to be both sovereign and good, would permit you to be taken from us. The events of your life are still easily and vividly called to mind from beginning to end.

Your mother telephoned me at work that it was time to take her to the hospital. As I sped to the hospital with her lying in the back seat, you began to come right along into the world. By the time we were at the hospital your feet were out. You had turned yourself around the wrong way again, even though we had just had you turned head down for delivery.

The delivering doctor was late and an emergency delivery was about to begin without him just as he arrived. The obstetrician scrubbed and went immediately to work. A nurse told me it was the fastest emergency Cesarean section delivery she'd ever seen. By the time I had completed the registration downstairs and come upstairs, you had already been born. You had three little spots of light hair on your head that one nurse called "angel's kisses." Your mother had feared that you had died during the delivery and these angel's kisses seemed a mark of some kind that we associated with almost losing you before birth on the way to the hospital and then during the emergency delivery, because your umbilical cord was wrapped around your neck. With all of the urgency, I forgot to buy your mother the dozen roses I'd planned to bring to her as I'd done when your sister was born.

The night after you were born I had a dream. I rarely remember my dreams and usually pay little attention to them even if I do recall them. That night I dreamed about you, little boy. My dream was vague but a roaring sound and blood were clear, and I had a sick, nauseating feeling with it. When I awoke, I felt in the dream that you died at a young age — probably in a motorcycle accident, which I associated with the roaring sound and the blood. I didn't tell anyone about this since I in no way felt sure it would happen. It seemed too strange and upsetting to tell.

I also felt the next day, for unknown reasons, that we should name you Daniel, which I later learned means "God is my judge," even though we had already agreed on the name Karl. The wish for a sudden change after much thought and discussion had gone into our choice of the name Karl was most unusual for me. Although these experiences at your birth were uncommon for me, I made nothing particular of them. They are more striking now looking back on it.

There were four of us now and your three-year-old sister was elated to have a baby brother. Your life progressed like that of any other baby's. You seemed just like any other baby and I suppose you were. Your fingers were so broad and your ears large. You were such a sturdy boy with a barrel chest and stocky ankles. You were a happy, smiling, drooling baby. We used to call you "the turtle" when you'd lie on your stomach in the carriage and push yourself up so that only your head could be seen over the side of the carriage. You loved to push yourself around the room in the little rolling baby walker. Watching your sister dance and jump, you would bubble with laughter and jump up and down on your mother's lap as you tried to dance too. Little boy, you seemed so alive and strong. When you stood in front of me at our evening prayers, you'd grasp one of my fingers with each hand as we would say, "Dear Father, hear and bless Thy beasts and singing birds, and guard with tenderness small things that have no words." We always thought of you as that "small thing that had no words."

We took you to see your grandparents in Denmark and there I spent more time with you than I had before. For reasons unknown to me, I hadn't seemed to attach as much to you as I had to your sister, and I had kept myself busy with work at night until this vacation. Your mother has said to me since learning of my dreams, that perhaps I was trying to avoid getting attached to you although I didn't realize it.

Trouble Begins

One Saturday morning, soon after returning from vacation, we got up early. At first you appeared your usual happy self, but later in the morning you seemed slightly ill and we suspected that you might have an ear infection. Nothing seemed out of the ordinary, but since I was planning to go to a convention on Monday, we decided to have you examined by the pediatrician that day, even though it was a Saturday, in case medication had to be started. You were seen by the pediatrician at 11 a.m. and an ear infection was diagnosed. Very routine — nothing unusual. The typical medicine was prescribed and begun. We put you to bed to nap. Your sister and I then went out for our Saturday romp while your mother watched over you with regular checks. I had the idea that today would be a good day to get the dozen roses for your mother that I'd forgotten the day you were born. We went to the florist and returned home and presented them to her. You were sleeping soundly and looked fine. I took your sister to the playground for a while. When we returned your mother and I checked on you again at about 4:30 as she had done while your sister and I were gone. Your breathing was deeper and more rapid, but your eyes twinkled and looked peaceful. You had a slight redness on your chest then, but nothing seemed striking about your appearance.

I've wondered since if you could have been rescued if we'd taken you back to the pediatrician then. Somehow we always want to know if there was anything that could have been done to avoid tragedy, but were told that it's most likely you would not have made it even if the illness had been recognized at 11 a.m. and that had you been rescued from death, you would have had substantial damage to your brain.

We put you back to nap some more. We checked you again soon. Your mother brought you from your crib. You were a deep blue. Her face was white. I found a faint pulse in you and gave you mouth-to-mouth resuscitation on the couch. I remember that your breath tasted and smelled pungent. I still can clearly taste that taste and smell the scent of your breath when I recall it.

We called the ambulance but before it arrived two deputy sheriffs came who had heard the call on their radio. They continued the

81

attempt to maintain you with mouth-to-mouth resuscitation. Your pulse was almost gone. The ambulance came. Suddenly it seemed that all of us were pushing furniture aside and they carried you out. I rode in the front of the ambulance. Your mother and sister followed in the car. As we rode I had the sense that this was what I'd dreamed of and that no one could keep your life with us from coming to an end. We arrived at the emergency room and were put in a small cubicle to wait while they worked on you. The nurse came finally and said that they'd managed to get air through to you. I was surprised and felt this wasn't the way it was supposed to go. I attribute no significance to my thoughts like this but they were a part of my experience at the time. A little past 8:30 p.m. another nurse came into the room and told us what I'd expected to hear — that despite great effort by the staff you could not fight off such a massive infection.

Death Comes Unexpectedly

At that moment there was in truth an absence of any feeling in me. Then a nurse told us that we could go and hold you to say good-bye to you. I held you for a few last minutes and talked to you. Then all the feelings broke through as I said how sorry I was that you wouldn't have more to your short life, that I would not be able to watch you grow through childhood into a young boy and then a man, that we could share no more together. We left the hospital, only the three of us, late that night. The many bright lights on the street as we left gave our leaving a feeling of unreality. The street seemed, for once, perfectly motionless except for us. We talked about you. We drove home. There was no sleep to be had by your mother and me that night. It was hard to absorb — hard to accept as real. The next morning your sister had forgotten what had happened. I told her again and we talked about it. Seeing your three-year-old sister try to understand that you were gone was almost as sad as the loss of you itself. The next day we called your grandparents and a few friends. We began to plan your funeral but an unbroken chain of visitors came the whole day and into the evening; neighbors and friends from church all came. They sat and talked. We told and retold the events of the past day uncountable times. By the end of Sunday we were still unable to eat. Finally, two good friends, a young physician and his wife, brought us some food and stayed to eat with us.

The next day the stream of visitors stopped. We had to go to the funeral home and choose the little box of a coffin for you to be left in. We chose your clothes too. Looking at the tiny blue shorts you would wear forever pounded the fact into me that you really had died. We were going to have your funeral and bury you. I went alone and watched them from a distance dig the hole to lay you in, and I wept.

The following day the funeral procession taking us to the church seemed to crawl in slow motion from the moment we sat in the car until the arrival at the church. During the worship service for you I felt most calm and at ease, as if everything was somehow all right with your leaving us. The hymns and scripture verses chosen by the minister fit together as if intended for each other. At the graveside we stayed to see the shovels close the earth around you. Then it seemed finished in a way. Yet it was not at all finished.

For days I walked through the graveyard searching to read what other parents had written on the tombstones, in part to keep company with them, in part to learn their secrets of how to look at losing you and how to live with it. Your mother and I must have made such a series of sad pictures as we came and stared at your grave. We came often to touch it because we could no longer touch you. We visited on all the special days for years. We came on Christmas, on your birthday, and on the anniversary of your death. We stood at your grave in the hot sun, we stood at your grave in the cold of winter, and we stood at your grave in the rain. That felt strangely good because it was as if the world cried with us then. We talked about you every night in the newly-found, awful quietness of our home. You weren't there anymore and you never would be. Each day and each evening this became more and more clear as we counted the days, weeks, and the months that had passed since you left us.

Christmas Eve in the dark I came to your grave and reached my hand down to touch the ground and felt a wreath of pine. I thought of how your mother's love still followed you in her making and placing of the wreath. I imagined that touching the needles was like being able to touch your hair. Your sister and I visited you at your grave every Saturday for months. We would have a soda together and talk about you. We all became very close — closer than we ever had been as we missed you together.

Searching For Meaning In His Life And Death

What can be said of his life or of his death? He enjoyed six months and three weeks and died quickly, painlessly it seemed. He left us in a state of incompleteness as if one leg of a four-legged stool was missing. I felt as if it were raining and stormy inside of me for months. I could not pray. My father sent me a cup with a rainbow on it. I had never thought much of it before but the story of Noah says the rainbow was a sign that God would never destroy the earth by flood again. The cup always seemed something good for me. It made me feel in some way my father's love for me.

Daniel was now another piece of me gone, it felt. Though I didn't believe there was a particular purpose in his death, thoughts went through my mind. Why did I want to change his name to Daniel (meaning "God is my judge")? Is there anything gained in the death of an innocent child somehow by the collective of humankind? Finally, I prayed to God, selfishly out of feeling cheated, that this loss could be made up to me now only by the birth of twin boys. This wish, which happened to come true, occupied my prayers. I am reluctant to claim that my prayer was answered as many might pray the same and have no more children. Others can discern what is to be made of this. I in no way find myself as meriting answered prayer. If we had had no more children, my view of God would, I hope, have been the same. That is that God is good. I tell this because there seems no reason to leave the odd things out. It happened that on the day of Daniel's first birthday following his death, my wife was scheduled for her first ultrasound after we learned she was pregnant. We discovered then on Daniel's birthday that we would have twins.

I sat in church the Sunday before the twins were born and sensed the awe that just one year and three days ago, from this church went the funeral train to bury our boy in the ground. Now we were to have two boys. How very strange. The twins were born one year and three days after Daniel's burial.

To God As The Blacksmith Of Souls

God, I feel it is you who is the Blacksmith of my soul as you pound and pound again with your unyielding and perfectly solid hammer while I lie against your immovable anvil. You pound with the recognition of the limits of my labor to produce anything approaching perfection. You pound with the limits of what can be had of wealth, power, and recognition. You tap lighter but are present still with the tedium of repetition of that which is necessary to keep life here maintained. You pound with the frustrations of crying children that I cannot satisfy despite my joy with them. I must reckon with the place of work as you pound and show me that I often cannot accomplish what I wish to and that what is accomplished seems lacking in significance. You pound deeply with the realization my mate and I will often thwart each other's happiness and seem unable to do otherwise.

For a while, God, I did not recognize it was you who was the real smithy in all of your disguises. As you know, I was always angry at the disguises — today's choice of hammer or even the anvil. After all, if the anvil would only give a little, perhaps the pounding would hurt less. But then I found you out. I have found you to be not only the Lord of Life, but also the Lord of Death. You pounded me with the death of a little boy I wanted to call mine, yet you would not have that be but for six months. I am no longer angry toward you now. Yet to have this little one slip as suddenly as sand between the fingers, to watch him fall with the same apparent inevitability as the leaf from the tree in autumn with nothing able to grasp onto his life, and for me to have had the night after his birth the thought, from nowhere it seemed, to change his name suddenly to that which means "God is my judge," and in a dream to hear noises, see blood, believe he'll die but sometime later in life, what can I make of this? The widow who told me that there would be a tender spot for him the rest of my life, I wished to brush aside. "Oh, no. I would be done with this as all else. She didn't

85

really know me so what could she know of this?" I thought. Yes, there is a spot but really a hole easily reopened. Since, as God, you are most powerful, it seems that certainly, had you desired it, the little boy would have lived. But he did not.

Who but you could remove us from our confident occupancy of a seat in the temple of this life and carefully place us each into the fire at just the right temperature for melting? You placed me in the fire, the melting heat of graveside visitations in the summer sun with his little sister left smiling by the granite lamb on the grave-stone, not understanding that the little one is gone, never to return. I see a child missing a child and me watching our little girl miss her baby brother. I want to call it a cruel trick, but I see no trick.

I visit the grave as if I could see the boy there. I stand with my wife but feel her to be more his mother and our silence to be not enough of a sharing despite talk at other times about him, about it, about us, but still not enough. I came on Christmas Eve after dark and felt in the cold air the pine wreath on his grave. I imagined that I had felt his hair when the needles passed between my fingers the way he passed between my fingers. The wreath made by the yet loving hand of his mother and laid there at his head to in some way care for him, to be his mother still. We visited that grave, that little tomb, at first every day, then every week, then on his birthday, the day of his death, the day of his funeral, and Christmas. We looked at the little stone of granite with the hand-carved lamb on top at sunrise, at noon, at sunset, at dusk, in the rain, and in the snow, watching others stand before this diminutive altar of sorts, talking to him, trying to hear what he would say back, not being able to talk to you, God, let alone sense what you would say back. The unexpected emotions at unforeseen times. It just all meant death — the death of anything and everything, the bursting forth of some occurrence of the whole never-ending story that still echoes.

Each event from the rush to the hospital on the day he was born, and the legs that emerged on the way to the emergency room, Cesarean section delivery done at lightning speed, to the three "angel's kisses" of small white spots in his dark hair come again and again to mind. His bones were so broad, so sturdy, and he was so happy for six months and three weeks. Those tiny strong legs, jumping as he watched his sister dance while his mother held him, are not forgotten. Nor is his laughter and glee or his peering over the baby carriage as he pushed himself proudly up.

To go and say good-bye to him dead, wrapped up in white cloths, the puncture holes to his throat and arm apparent, to hold him dead and feel that he is there but gone, was ours to do. I was afraid that if I didn't hold him an essential moment would be forever gone. Yes, you pounded with that hammer for so long with thudding blows but the first three days brought the sharpest, most penetrating and shaking strokes as we chose the clothes our little one would always wear. Looking at the blue shorts with straps and the shirt laid out across our bed, it seemed a knife from somewhere went through my stomach and slit it with an upward thrust. Then it broke or perhaps I broke on the anvil of the bed as I fell forward across it and in rage brought my fists down to the mattress as if I could somehow be like you and feel some power. But there was no power — only the give of the mattress under the clothes that seemed to be looking at me.

It must be that you remember us in the fire to retrieve our remnant so that we might tremble once more at your mighty arm as you hammer anew. You hammered with fear before entering the funeral home the first time. What would be inside? You hammered and hammered with each shovel of dirt as the diggers hollowed out the resting place to tuck him in. You hammered each time there was the sound of the iron shovel scraping against the rock when it cut into the earth just as inside I was scraped and cut as I listened and watched them work on the ground while you worked on me, beating through to my insides and then pounding on them.

There was no interest in food and no ability to sleep. You did permit us soothing friends at least, to cool us before you allowed our remnants to tremble once more under your mighty arm.

Although I sensed at his funeral that we were the object of pity for this large gathering, and it was undeniably pitiable, I felt your comfort and peace around me. Perhaps I was too tired, too wrung out and depleted to feel anything else. At the graveside after the awkward procession of greeters came by us, each understandingly uncomfortable with whatever was said in this procession more solemn than at the funeral home two nights before. This was the prelude to the finality as the dirt was shoveled over the toy-like coffin. This was the beginning of being placed into the fire again.

It was a fire of knowing that clock time was passing but experiencing the heaviness of a time that did not seem to pass as if clock time ran the daytime world outside of the house, but at home in the evenings there was only the never-ending now, unmoving with its weight. This hammer of time that you use in different ways — bending, twisting as if with forceps, then rolling out and pinching in the vise — you will not let go. I think of the hymn sung at his funeral, "Oh Love That Will Not Let Me Go." Is this a part of your love? Is this what I have read of as a "severe mercy"? Certainly this is the severest of mercies if it is somehow a mercy and this "joy that seekest me through pain" as the hymn reads — somehow I haven't felt the joy just now. I can't quite sing the words "death" or "dying." My eye finds them ahead and keeps me from them while I shake as others sing. I can't honestly believe the hymn's lyrics, "I give thee back the life I owe," since the one gone is only mine by way of attachment, and I certainly did not give him up willingly. I must conclude that you took him or you allowed him to be taken. Is there a real difference? I wonder, and only you would know how much of all of this grief is really for him and how much is for some other losses — the loss of my youth, the loss of my physical capabilities, or even the losses that I do not focus on from my own childhood.

I hear another line from the hymn, "Oh cross that liftest up my head, I dare not ask to fly from Thee." No, I dare not ask for you to leave me alone. Severe or not, you are the only smithy of souls. Even Jesus said, "The cup which my father has given me, shall I not drink it?" So who am I to protest even if I, like him, might ask that the cup be taken from me? Too, if he wept and was "deeply moved inwardly," should that be strange for me or for us?

Wandering in the graveyard I look for something I cannot find in you. How did these others whose children are buried here feel and think about it and about you? I look for them to speak to me in the words they leave on the stone in that final closing statement.

There are more children's graves than I'd imagined. Most are from generations ago. Six stones in a row show a father and five children all having lived to somewhere between infancy and middle age. I see that you have left a woman almost one hundred years old to see the death of her husband and five children. She is not here. I assume she lives nearby and carries on in this life. She has just unknowingly helped me — given me courage and a challenge. There is one other that struck me. Two small stones side by side show two young girls, sisters, are buried there. Six months after the first, the second was taken. Surely, you drove a rivet and then a spike into these parents. They inscribed on the gravestone for the first, "He who loves our little girl more than we, has called her home." A faithful enough expression for a lifetime but on the second stone was written, "God gave. He has taken. He will restore. He doeth all things well." To have such love and hopeful attachment to you even when the attachment to their children in the here and now was broken — how could they? No anger is here, just confidence that somehow the course of life and of death is being done well by you who does all things well. That is, if you did it, then it is done well and perfectly. No matter if it seems it must be bad, wrong, or even evil — if it is by your hand, then it is done well.

Pound, pound, and pound again. Though I feel I am either to break or be punctured I seem to be being made more solid and yet reshaped as if my character were in part being forged again. It is as if the pounding is to work on the soul despite the personality that the soul is trapped in. God, did you make us as souls trapped in personalities such that we must look beyond the personality in order to meet as souls? Must we overlook much of the personality to be capable of loving the most perfect and most central parts of another person? Does this mechanism, this tool called personality, despite its best efforts, create obstacles to love? It is helpless to help itself. There is a discomfort in all of this. I want to ask: Did you set the world in motion and us with it in such a way that we can glimpse a sense of what the most perfect might be like so that we chase after it in many forms only for those forms to become your hammers that have been hidden from our view as to their true nature? Do you orchestrate all of this so that it frustrates and pains us that we might be driven to you?

It seems you do things like take people from Mars called men and people from Venus called women and have them placed on earth together where they must get along. They desire each other, but with your wiring us differently and placing our brains in different baths of chemicals, we seem to have some abyss between us that is recognized more with age though we may try to understand the other with effort and sincerity. It is as if those who give life through birth and nurturance and those who take life through crime and war must somehow reconcile, must somehow live together. Is this a reflection of your being — a force-unto-life to create and a force-unto-death to destroy? Disease, tidal waves, earthquakes, and hurricanes are known even as "acts of God." Yes, you are the giver and the taker. But then can I say to you the giver, it is not yours to take? And can I believe that somehow all this taking, all this destruction and death, disease and decay is not actually "evil" because it is yours? Can I believe that it is me who does not see? Do we become evil as we assume the force-unto-death or is that our prerogative too at times though we are not the giver? Even if I do not take the life I did not give, in my anger I take the moment I did not give. I cannot deny the potential of the force-unto-death. I could use it if I thought I must to protect my child or even myself. I say that I am yours but would not turn the other cheek while being killed, or so I think. What does that make me? The poet asked of the tiger — "Did He who made the lamb make thee?" What is this perfect paradox — the tiger and the lamb, the force of creation and the force of destruction, man and woman? Is it God alone? Is it God and the Evil One or God and the evil that springs from the human heart? Well, you made it all. Did you somehow make something you did not intend? Is the Evil One a "one" within the heart of each of us? Is it evil to assume the prerogative of the force-unto-death and to resist you? Is it a need or wish not to need you, a wish to have the belief of "No-God" and to react against God and the idea of God with anger, a sense of self derived from asserting ultimate, complete, and final separation and autonomy from all else, persons and you? Did you create me and all persons knowingly with the temptation to act so? As God, you must have, but the reason seems imponderable. Since I do not reject you, I must have the tension between the fright and the joy of losing myself in you. Would you leave much or any of me remaining as I go (or is it actually as I am drawn) to dissolve like a drop in the ocean?

But can I resist you, the only smithy of souls, and not lose the care of my soul entirely? Must we lie under your mighty arm until we see no self in self or others but only the sea of molten souls on your anvil as they are seen by the eye of the Forger? Oh, Lord, once you may have been the Potter and we the clay, but now, surely, you are the Blacksmith of our souls as you strike and strike again. How can we leave you if a solid sense of peace is found only in you? The peace, if it is that, from all else seems but infatuation by comparison and all else, even the love of a child, leaves with the passing of persons. You, God, whatever you are, you are at least all that endures.

Are you really the God who authored the death by excruciatingly painful means of the one who is called your son? How can this be a holy and a perfect plan? It seems you had no regard for his suffering. At least you deemed it necessary for some other good. Do you deem the same for us? Is this that we call "suffering" intentional? I know the scripture reads that we are like a woman in childbirth, in pain now but that pain is said to be forgotten once it is past. Does that mean that the pain of repeated "nows" is unimportant by comparison to the goal — whatever that goal is? Yes, you let him suffer even though he cried out to you. Was this actually your crying out to yourself? Then a part of you authored the crucifying of the rest of you. Is that what this is about for us too? We are left only to guess. An interesting trick itself so that in order to come to you we must go beyond the observations of the senses alone and believe that there is more here. This first step of faith seems to require putting the self as a self-second and believing in more than what the self can directly grasp. We must go beyond the senses and reason at the outset and find something in another part of us. Then ultimate faith in the senses and the capacities of the self alone would seem to die. Is that a beginning of part of the self crucifying another part — something dying, something born?

91

You, yourself, are perhaps the greatest mystery if this world is your creation and is in some way a reflection of you. I had wanted to see you as some familiar form — maybe something my parents told me about — but you will not be as predictable. You seem always to come to me as a stranger just as the priest and the Levite passed the beaten man by. Then you came as a stranger, a foreigner, or even an outcast. Always forcing me to stretch my picture of you to encompass the new, bigger, more complete, and then more mysterious in its wonderment, experience of you. I suppose I haven't really found you until I've left the picture given by my parents behind in favor of what I find. It seems that if their picture of you is just like mine then I've let them be too much of my image of you, and the picture of them remains in part where you should be. But only you know.

Suffering, Sacrifice, And God

For some reason that is perhaps intended to elude us, God seems to have constructed the world so that there is pain and suffering from so-called "natural occurrences" as well as from acts of destruction or evil done by us ourselves. It seems impossible to imagine why. Perhaps the why is unimportant as compared to our response. Can we still love the God with whom we are angry for not having created the world differently? If so, how much more is that love since it is in spite of pain and loss? If I can still love this God who permits such things to happen, are not my fears and resentments then bound up and contained by and in that love? This would be akin to the love for our parents that binds and contains the feelings of anger and hostility for real or perceived wrongs done by them to us. When both love and anger are felt towards the same being, the feelings of love can bind and transform the anger and allow forgiveness.

Are not our particular character and whatever contribution we may make to this world in part a product of what we have endured and how we have endured it? If so, then without whatever pain we have experienced the contribution that is or will be ours would at least have been different. Does the way we live with the pains that come our way effect changes in some spirit or soul within us as

92

Soren Kierkegaard thought? I have come to the belief that it does; if this is so then we endure travail for a good reason.

I often think of the story of how Abraham was asked to sacrifice Isaac, his long-awaited son, to God in order to show that he still had primary loyalty to God alone. Did Abraham think this was strange if not horrible? What kind of image of God does this show? The God of Abraham seems, on the whole, more concerned with what happened to this group of his people than with any individual.

This doesn't suit our individualistic mentality. We seem to feel that each of us as separate individuals must have some special, unique significance. In this story of Abraham, as in other biblical stories, we see that the particular sufferings or pains of a given individual appear to be not as important as what happens to the group or what happens as a demonstration of God working his intentions in history. Though Moses had been a great and faithful leader for the most part, he was not chosen to actually lead the people to their final destination. God is not portrayed as feeling pangs of guilt at withholding this from Moses as parents of today might. Yet we might imagine that God could have felt sympathetic with Moses in his disappointment. As a Being, the God of the Old Testament does not seem concerned with whether he is liked, but rather he is concerned with whether he is loved with a fidelity and devotion that leads to a carrying out of his purposes. At times it can almost seem as if this God wants to prompt people to do any number of things that we would consider strange or unreasonable, just to see if the people will do them. It appears from one perspective that God wished to see if people would go against that which is usually most precious to human beings, their reasoning ability, and follow him with a blind and complete trust into "unreasonableness." Perhaps this is the greatest test of trust and belief we can face.

The God of Jesus seems in some ways the same. It was more important that the crucifixion of Jesus take place than that Jesus avoid pain and suffering. This pain and suffering were a part of God's purpose with people. Like Abraham and Isaac, the story of how God is sacrificing Jesus has always struck me as strange. If we think about this a while, we may not like this God's way of operating with the sacrifice of a son, who, in spite of being fully divine, is nevertheless still supposed to be fully human and hurt just as you and I would.

Reason, Suffering, And Belief

Jesus is to follow God into what is certainly, by our view, "unreasonable." If this was to be Jesus' purpose in the world ordained by God, then how truly chosen by Jesus was it? Despite the writings about Jesus recognizing and accepting his Messiahship, the actual degree of his choice regarding the events of his life remains unknown to us. The way God is to have acted with Jesus shows God to be more concerned with the larger picture than with whatever agony Jesus went through. This may seem a harsh God to us.

I have come to like the depiction of God as "emptying" a part of himself into Jesus. In a sense a son is a part of the self emptied into another being. With this way of looking at it, when God offers his son as a sacrifice, he is offering a part of himself. Many will conclude there is no difference and perhaps that is so, but to me one emphasizes God's offering another being as a sacrifice more than it emphasizes his offering himself. Either way, a part of the Being of God is to follow itself into what would appear to be unreasonableness, and this is happening for the benefit of others.

The vengeful, wrathful image of a God of harsh justice has kept many away from the God of Jesus. If we emphasize the separateness of the Being of Jesus from the Being of God, then God can appear to have a sense of justice that is too harsh since he authored and permitted Jesus' pain. If we emphasize the union of the Being of Jesus and the Being of God, then we can see a God who empties himself into human form and, rather than wanting sacrifices to be made to him, offers himself as the sacrifice.

Once when I was completely paralyzed on the left side of my body and in a wheelchair, my father said to me that if there was any way he could have taken this disability on himself and thereby taken it from me, he would have done so. What can I ever say to this? It is purely and simply the same self-giving *agape* love I have come to believe that God has for us. In order for us to contain our potential for the self-centered destruction of each other and ourselves and to transform our endless desiring that fuels the evil we do, such a self-sacrificing God, with whom we can identify and then imitate, may be essential.

This is the God who would take the pains of the world onto himself by emptying his essence into the form of a human. He comes to us as he came to the Jewish people, first as a baby, innocent and in need of our care as all such little ones do. As a baby he does not frighten us but compels our affections. Likewise, he comes to us as he came to the Greeks, the *Logos*, "the principle of reason," become flesh. He then compels us with his wisdom and his actions that would lead us into "unreasonableness" by purely rational standards of thinking were we to believe his teachings are true. So, we cannot believe them until we no longer trust the perfection of our reasonableness.

The heroics of this Jesus show us a blameless one who lived out the death of a criminal. The death of the self-centered self is slow and painful, as was his, but it allows the self now centered in the *agape* love of God to rise. Jesus is able then to forgive those who have tortured him since Jesus' devotion to God was complete. He had no self-centered self. Yet he dies the death of self-centered ones who because of their very self-centeredness have done evil. He dies then, a death he did not deserve. This Jesus shows us the drops of blood of one who is innocent of the crime dripping to the ground. He shows this death for us that we might learn to put to death our own self-centeredness and thereby end the cycle of death and suffering that we continue with our violence and destruction. He, who was perfectly contained by God's *agape* love and who contained in himself a part of the essence of God, dies that we might also be contained by God's *agape* love having sacrificed our self-centeredness. Contained in God's *agape* love we are enabled to be a catalyst to transform evil instead of perpetuating it.

What other than this holy, perfect *agape* love activated in our being can contain our rage and aggression and save us from ourselves? He who was most perfect sacrifices himself to show us the way of self-sacrifice, to show us the God of self-sacrifice who would have us reject the reasonableness of the obvious and the self-centered and become united with him in the way of self-sacrifice.

What is this pain, this loss, all of the pains and losses for all of us about? Given how God himself chose to teach us by way of a crucifixion, it seems hard to believe that God values human flesh, emotions, or thought in the same self-interested way that we usually do. We would cling to it whereas God has shown himself to be prepared to permit the sacrifice of bodies and feelings in the service of something greater. We, by our sacrifices and perhaps by our sufferings, may become part of this greater something. What is this that is greater? I doubt that we like the possibility that God may be working to perfect our spirits or souls. We probably will not consider that he may permit sufferings to bring us to him and to each other. What we see as suffering then is perhaps preparatory work.

"Well, why then?" we ask. But we don't necessarily get a reply and we don't like this at all. We at least want an explanation if we must put up with all of the frustration, the losses, the pain, the anxiety, and the death, but we are left only able to ask, "Why couldn't it have been another way?" Perhaps the bond between us is greater when fused by pain or when fused by pain that is contained by love. Perhaps our bond to God is likewise strengthened when it is forged in both pain and love.

I have been told by noteworthy scholars and theologians that we must not think of a God who is good as even intentionally permitting tragedy and human pain and that certainly we cannot think God would ever directly cause us to suffer in order that we might somehow become better. Our good God would choose another way of teaching us. This may be the case. However, can we so confidently assume it is certainly the case? True, it may provide more consolation for some victims of tragedy to say that our God is too good to permit or excuse such pain intentionally. Is this being honest with ourselves? If we assume there is a demonic power to account for that which we say was neither caused by the human hand nor by the divine hand, then doesn't God permit this demonic power? We still will ask, "Why?"

What would a world without suffering be like? Would we find any need for God there? Would there be any evil? Could there be a self-sacrifice that willingly takes suffering on? If nota then is it likely this is not a universe created by a God whose character is of self-sacrifice and who wishes to bring the world to him in this way? Do we have a God who wants us to struggle with our self-giving capabilities to contain and transform our self-getting preoccupation by self-giving? We at least want an explanation if we must put up with all of the frustration, the losses, the pain, the despair, and the death. But we are left only able to wonder, "Why couldn't it have been another way?"

Chapter 7

The Pain And Gain In Psychotherapy And In Life

The Nature Of God As Experience Might Suggest

It seems that just as human beings have a capacity for rage and to kill for self-protective purposes, this aggressive, destructive capacity in its less extreme forms can also be used in the service of solely self-centered motives. It appears, too, that God has the capacity at least to permit that which is horrible, tragic, or evil as we see it. At a minimum God has a capacity to permit destruction and death and it is possible that God may use an active capacity to destroy for some greater good. Yet since God by virtue of being God could sense no threat to his Being as humans might, God's capacity to destroy would not be ruled by rage in response to threat, and God's capacity to destroy can be seen as bound and contained by *agape* love. Since it would be completely contained by *agape* love, God's destructive capacity could not be "self-centered" or ultimately "bad." As the Deity, perfect and holy, God's intentions are beyond good and beyond human judgment.

Our grief from a sense of loss in life must not be glossed over. However, after honest grieving has been accomplished, our question in response to pain must relinquish the demand for an answer to "why" and engage the "what." That is, "What can be done now *with* that which has happened to me in order to honor and serve God best?" This is the same question we must come to ask when not in pain.

The possible answers to "why" are in large part constructed from the "what" of our response. We are to a great extent made up of that which happens to us and the marks it leaves. Anything done with the effects of those marks generates some meaning about the experience that left the marks. Sheldon Vanauken in his book *A Severe Mercy* elaborates on this title phrase coined by the writer C. S. Lewis in their correspondence. The phrase does not deny the pain resulting from the loss, but the interpretation of the loss is put in a context of meaning that casts all of human experience in relation to a sovereign, loving God. This God may permit or cause that which is severe to come our way. Yet these experiences can be believed to be, or to become, "mercies" in some way. However, the particulars may need to be discovered as life progresses and may take much time. The loss must come to be seen in the context of new experiences in life. Not to trust God in this way may be to assume that God's nature is no more than human nature.

Alternatively, the particulars may forever elude us as to how a particular severe experience is nevertheless a mercy. This is an occasion for the challenge to believe and to trust in spite of the apparent unreasonableness of doing so. This is when faith becomes the most that it can be. This is when conviction in that which is beyond the immediate world can take us beyond ourselves. This is when unreasonableness, grounded in that which transcends us, can do in our human lives what reason alone can never do. Thought, feeling, and action converging on a hope in the future can lift us from the present to begin a life now that is beyond and above ourselves. In this process we become transformed by belief and hope interacting with elements above and beyond human existence such that when tomorrow has become yesterday even our past has been transformed. As such beings, we begin to live outside of time and in the domain and dimension of hope and new possibilities grounded in God's eternity.

This is the hope and trust exemplified by the parents who, at the death of their little daughter, left the gravesite epitaph, "He who loves our little girl more than we, has called her home." We ask how they could write this. It is unimaginable that some months later at the death of their second little girl they could write, "God has given. He has taken. He will restore. He doeth all things well." We may be able to believe that "God has given." I suggest that because we will not say at times that it is God who has taken, we then cannot believe that God will restore and that it is God who, in fact, does all things well. Since any destruction by God is merciful it cannot be self-serving. Humans, on the other hand, are most

100

capable of being self-servingly destructive and desirous in our actions even when it would not appear necessary. We, in a part of ourselves, seem to love to triumph over each other in one way or another. This destructive aspect appears to be intertwined with our desire always to have more of something since we will destroy for personal gain. Our endless desirousness might be viewed as the urge to enlarge the self by satisfying our desire and appetite for more which can be contained only by placing the self in the service of some larger, more enduring, and more perfect other or cause. Such service also provides a way to outlive ourselves as the larger other goes on after we die. However, losing the self in service requires renouncing the enlargement of ourselves by the satisfaction of our desires to acquire more. Both are ways to silence our hidden fears of our own death, inadequacy, ambivalence, or lack of meaning in life.

The most enduring, most perfect, most potent "other" is God. By looking at the self as God might see us, we have the possibility to rise above the smallness of our usual perspective on life. In so doing we gain the option of truly enlarging ourselves to the greatest degree possible, yet that comes about by the loss, dilution, or transformation of the self in the Being of God and God's intentions. Only the God of self-sacrifice and *agape* love has shown us how we can be contained and then live free of the evil we would do to each other. The transformation of the self-centered self to the self of *agape* love can come about only by desiring this *agape* love above all other desires. This requires the sacrifice of the self which is something so unreasonable that many of us will make the sacrifice only for a God who has done so for us and who asks us to do likewise. Because of God's self-giving love for us and the call to love unselfishly in return, we can be motivated to live in the spirit of this love.

To love the God of *agape* love with all of my body, soul, mind, and strength is to love God more than I love myself — no small task. It is to attempt to see myself as God would see me and to discern how this God would have me be. In desiring this *agape* love most, my self no longer lives primarily to gratify my self-absorbed wishes. Then, the self living only for its own sake is lost.

If I love my neighbor as myself in radical and complete *agape* love, I recognize no distinction in the relative weight of my neighbors' needs and of my own. Must I lose myself so entirely as a separate self? If I am but a "branch on the vine" I am not the major piece nor am I seeking to determine my own direction of growth insofar as I am attached to the vine. My selfhood is again eclipsed.

If I drink of the water which will make me never thirst again and if I eat of the bread that eternally fills, must I not see my complete reliance on the God who takes the place of whatever I depended on before? If I permit my feet to be washed, must I not then wash the feet of others? Where is the boundary of my self? Where is the individual — the separateness? When I am in the Light of Life do I have a shadow? I then recognize that I cannot transform myself as an independent self and can do so only to the degree that I both choose to and to the degree that I stand at the door of the unseen and knock, seeking constant help from the God on whom I acknowledge my complete and unreserved dependence. It is in this vein that I can believe that in grasping my life too tightly as my own that I shall lose it because I will be left alone since it is only "my" life, with all of the aloneness and isolation such a life brings. Such a life is empty of any meaning except that which I dream is true within my self-centered self.

To believe that you would never feel the wish for perfection and that if you did you would renounce it as infantile or foolish without any quest for it, to be certain that you would never experience a sense of terror or frightening bodily reactions beyond your control, to believe that you or one you love will never be seriously debilitated physically, or to be confident that you will never have to do something like bury your child, is to avoid seeing that life itself and all that is within it hangs by a few threads for each of us. Yet believing these realities are active possibilities is most difficult apart from some context of meaning that renders the associated anxiety tolerable. Until we have a way of accepting such fearsome possibilities we will live in a state of denial about them, characterized by minimizing the likelihood of something terrible happening to us personally. Unless we reckon with these possibilities as despairing, frightening, or troubling as they may be, it is probable that we will avoid confronting the necessity of having a context of meaning that will enable us to live through the trauma human life can become. Said another way, having experiences that seem intolerable, as we now see human life, may make it more likely that we will come to a different understanding of human life. That understanding might be in relation to a sovereign but loving God who may author but who certainly permits what we may see as tragic, evil, bad, terrible, or horrible. The severity of these experiences and our responses to them can then seem to require strengthening company with the Creator as the Higher Power who can foster transformation in us.

To believe that humankind with the exertion of will and reason can overcome all of its problems rooted in and caused by profound loss and the consequent feelings or those problems caused by self-centered greed and aggression is to deny that the source of our problems is in the very nature of each of us. Such a belief is also a display of the desires and inflated sense of self we would claim to be able to master, given that much of our recorded history is a testament to the insatiability of humanity's self-centered desires. The most complete transformation of a human being must begin with the death of self-centeredness that then opens us to the greatest of possibilities and the greatest of realities.

The Pain Of Change

An individual's pain is, so to speak, the gas in the tank for psychotherapy. I believe that our pain is also much of the gas in the tank for our potential change and possible transformation that can be realized in life as a whole. It is the fear of pain and loss that keeps us from doing what we might do; thus this fear is the substance of our resistance and reluctance to change. This stalemate situation may be viewed in terms of conflicting fears (e.g. I fear moving and I fear not moving), conflicting wishes (e.g. I wish to move and I wish not to move), or conflicting wishes and fears (e.g. I wish to move, but if I do I fear the expense and I wish not to move but I fear the decreasing property value here). What this amounts to is that we, like most who engage in psychotherapy, initially want the benefits of the change without experiencing the pain and the

103

loss of something. We want change without risking the pain from loss and the tolerance of anxiety required for personal transformation. Life is made up of change. This sounds so simple. Coping with external change requires inner change or transformation. Psychotherapy is made up of possible changes and a changing dance around this potential. Life and psychotherapy are ultimately processes of letting go of what has been in order to change and adapt to what is or what might be. Somehow our seeing what *is* must be reconciled with the sight of what was or what we have always thought *ought* to be. We are not giving up "ought." We are reconsidering it and redefining it to adequately include *is*. This involves letting go of or diminishing the wishes and the fears that have guided us thus far. We are letting pieces of what we believe to be our SELF go at each juncture of development. Actually, we are letting go of the pictures, images, ideas, and beliefs we have had about our SELF, so much so that across the span of development in life, we eventually have different senses of the SELF until it becomes a self. And thus we become less SELF-centered in order for the self to adapt in the world.

This letting go may evoke periods of grief including tears, and often we do not know why we are crying when we are grieving the losses inherent in change. I have worked with people who upon graduation from college or professional school or upon reaching the age of thirty, forty, or fifty have had uncontrollable crying spells. They are in a state of profound transition and therefore a state of identity shift. They are not just depressed. They are grieving a loss or an anticipated loss. But life and psychotherapy are in part about letting go of what is or what seems to be in order to embrace that which is becoming. We may need to hang on to parts of the present in order to proceed into the future. There is no problem in that. When that fragment of this present sense of self becomes useless or unnecessary, it will fall by the wayside.

Almost every problem that people bring in the door when they come to see me as a psychologist seems to be linked with wanting not to change or to let go of something in order to obtain what they say they want. For example, I've seen many people who wish to be rid of headaches. Frequently we conclude that the headaches come about when people avoid doing a particular thing, such as being appropriately and kindly assertive in speaking their mind or standing up for themselves. Usually the people avoid doing this because they greatly fear that if they do speak more candidly, they will not be well liked. Further, they generally feel that they must be very well liked by all people at all times, and that they will not be able to tolerate it if they aren't liked by everyone. Such people may feel that they will be somehow punished or rejected for standing up for their own thoughts and wishes and that they could not live well enough with this rejection if it occurred at all, ever. They are stuck because they will not risk the loss of being so well liked. It often appears that they are so dependent on the approval of others that treating themselves as well as they treat others is impossible. At some level of the mind this is probably resented. However, people with this difficulty may also feel that it is wrong for them to be at all resentful and angry. Then they must hide these feelings even from themselves. This ball of inner conflict and tension can easily result in a headache.

Of course, people develop these fears for some reason and the headaches may have served a function in the past. Perhaps this is the best adaptation to their life circumstances that they could find as a child. Nevertheless, as an adult now and no longer as truly dependent on parents as a child, they cannot be as easily victimized as a child. Perhaps they are experiencing some gain or "pay off" at times for maintaining this fearful child-like position in life.

Gaining some insight into how the pattern developed might be helpful, but the dependency on others will eventually need to be let go of. This is an opening for the theological psychologist. If this dependency can be shifted to God or a Higher Power, then the courage to change may be found. In a sense such a move directs feelings of dependency toward where they, I would say, belong for an adult.

This highlights a critical difference in a theological psychology and humanistic psychology. The latter would say we have not assumed full adulthood until we are dependent primarily on ourselves alone; the theological psychologist asserts that it is our very nature to look beyond ourselves and to God as the final source on whom we depend. To let the opinions of others carry ultimate and final weight as to how we feel about ourselves is to let them be as a god to us. Finding a real Higher Power who affirms us despite limitations can be helpful in prompting change and be constructive as a resource too while developing and adapting. Yet something "in hand," so to speak, must be let go of. That is frightening, but it is made easier with God to hold onto with the other hand.

Finding The Meaning For Living In Another Person

It is common in my practice to have people come to me who have just been rejected by their spouse or partner. They wish to be over the pain of losing the partner. Yet they frequently do not want to surrender what appears to be an idealization or an exaggeration of the perfection of the other person. They do not want to surrender the process of idealizing another as a way to come by their meaning in life. In the process of idealization, a person acts towards another as if he or she is "at least ten feet tall" so that praise from this idealized other person carries the weight of praise from a parent to a young child. It has a near god-like quality to it. Then, so too does the criticism or rejection by this other carry with it a larger-than-life quality.

When a relationship that has been characterized by idealization ends, there is not only the loss of a person that one is attached to that must be reckoned with, there is also the loss of a connection with something ideal which provided a deeper meaning than an attachment alone does. In some sense the one who idealizes feels more ideal too, by way of his or her association with the other. Therefore, a decrease in self-esteem also comes about when the idealized attachment is broken. Hence, there is a loss of self-esteem in addition to the loss of the attachment. There may also be a loss of meaning in life due to the loss of the one who is idealized.

It is probable that when a person is idealized to the point that the meaning in life and self-esteem of another are derived from the relationship, the idealizer has made this other person a little god of sorts. Idealizing that which does not actually transcend human life or wishing to be seen in an idealized way would seem to make such relationships an attempt to give, receive, or exchange admiration instead of an effort to love born of a mutual concern for the other's well-being. Idealizing only that which does in fact transcend human experience makes it less likely that we will worship a human being and feel that our wholeness and value as a person depends upon being connected in some way to a particular person. This is in no way to deny or minimize all of the more psychological reasons and causes for such idealizing. However, we do tend to idealize something. If that something is God, who by definition cannot be accurately de-idealized (though we may be angry at God or disappointed in God), then perhaps we are less likely to idealize other human beings. If the other person has not been idealized, we will deal with the loss of attachment rather than the loss of meaning, self-esteem, or the loss of some being we worship when a romantic relationship ends. We wish to be over the pain from the loss of romance without rejecting having a relationship with someone we idealize as a means to fill our own inner void.

We wish to avoid the pain and anxiety of our inner emptiness and void, but we are not willing to experience this emptiness and void long enough to discover what we must do to master it and to fill it. Instead we focus our pain or anxiety on some smaller task and make a god of something, which in turn becomes like an addiction because we keep needing more to numb the gnawing of the void. Yet we feel that there can never be enough of what we want because what we are really seeking is more than the particular thing we are consciously desiring. It is a substitute and an idol of sorts. We are like a bucket with a hole in it that is unable to be filled by what we are now desiring. Even our own physical appearance or occupational success can become this mini-god. We wish to be over the fear of appearing to be horrible or inadequate. Yet we will not let go of the wish to appear wonderful in order to do so. Fearing one appears horrible is almost always tied to the wish to appear wonderful. Such an individual may wish to become like a mini-god and attempt to substitute the admiration and envy, bordering on worship, of others for honest love and intimacy which includes mutuality in vulnerability.

We wish to have no limits on what we can do and what we can have, but we fear, perhaps largely outside of our conscious awareness, the lack of being contained and hence bounded by something. We fear this because somewhere in ourselves we sense that we are terribly small and not up to taking on all by ourselves the vast universe in which we reside. We wish for no limits but fear unknowingly that we will then have no bounds, since having no bounds means we have no container and therefore no protection. We resist giving up the wish for no limits and accepting God as the definer of our boundaries and our limits despite the fact that we are unable, unless we engage in massive denial or make a god of something else, to abandon the fear of our own nothingness up against the universe.

We wish to feel that we are in control of this world or at least that we are in control of our own lives, but we simultaneously fear the risks with this responsibility. We fear being responsible for a bad outcome. We struggle to be in control in part because its opposite — feeling helpless, and the correlate sense of futility — is so terribly troublesome. It is often to avoid feelings of despair and hopelessness that one expresses frustration in the form of violent rage. This at least wards off feelings of impotence and futility. To acknowledge that I have no control or very little control in a particular situation also engenders a sense of loss. Then the belief that I can be an effective agent of change at all times and in all places is compromised. This belief and therefore a part of my sense of myself and the world die to an extent when I accept the limited amount of control I have.

Learning To Let Go In Order To Live

Growth, progression, and development in life inevitably require loss since with every move toward something there is a corresponding move away from something else. Therefore, providing some meaning to these losses with possible, if not probable, reasons suggesting why the losses are at least acceptable is truly essential if we are not to become bitter and angry, avoidant, fearful, despairing, despondent, apathetic, and resigned in life. Lack of experiential living in relatedness with others and with the elements,

108

coupled with denial, work together to mitigate against the conclusion that reckoning with loss is essential. The lack of this reckoning leads to misery of some sort. The need to let go of something in order to change is illustrated in the story told earlier of "The Chinese Monkey Trap."

Much of such letting go has to do with accepting losses concerning the probable limits on who we are and what we will become without placing limits on our efforts concerning who we might become. So a rosebud, even with much strenuous effort, can never grow into a tulip, but it may then become a less fully developed rose. Yet a rosebud with little, if any, effort can become a beautifully blossoming rose. Why the roses and tulips are there and how they are planted, only the gardener knows. Some of the losses in life are inevitable due to our own ambivalence and inner conflict and can be well characterized by metaphors for the dilemmas. For example, the story of a little boy reaching out toward a goose as if to pet it but then realizing that the goose might bite him. The boy's hand pictured frozen in space illustrates that he is stuck since he cannot decide what he wants to do most. His wish to pet the goose is exactly and proportionally balanced by his fear of being bitten if he does pet the goose. Although psychologists most often look at this as a conflict between a wish and a fear or the inclination to approach versus the inclination to avoid, it is quite accurate to look at the dilemma in terms of anticipated loss. The little boy must choose to lose either his sense of safety or his sense of enjoyment.

This picture might become more complicated if a duck were to walk onto the scene; the boy may wish to pet them both and fear petting them both. However, to the observer it might simply appear that he didn't know which one he wanted to pet although in truth he actually would be afraid to pet either. In the case of a person who can't decide which potential romantic interest to pursue, it is quite possible that the person is afraid to pursue either to the point of a commitment being made. Making such a commitment also requires the acceptance of a loss — the loss of being uncommitted and the loss of being committed to any other potential partner.

109

L. L. Constantine in the book *Family Paradigms: The Practice Of Theory In Family Therapy*, writes that "all family problems are the result of unresolved grief in connection with a past loss." I would suggest that it is accurate to say that all non-organically based psycho-emotional problems are at least in part the result of a failure to accept and incorporate adequately past or anticipated losses in a way that still leaves one optimistic about life. It is not yet clear that a therapy focused on constructively reckoning with the inevitable and the particular losses in life would not be of use with these organically-based illnesses too as an adjunctive treatment.

The theological solution offers a unique way to live with losses in life without resorting to despair or denial. In a sense the theological solution may be inevitable if we watch life in and around us. Nothing else seems to offer an adequate, comprehensive view of what life presents us with and still ends up with hope for the future.

Putting It All Together

Human beings have a destructive capacity which, though existing for the purpose of material self-preservation, is often used to fortify the sense of the potency of the self. It may also be used in the service of acquiring some material gain to enlarge the sense of self-adequacy. Such acts are often done to keep at a distance feelings of anxiety and frustration with regard to our fears that life may be meaningless and ourselves insignificant, and the associated painful feelings of loss. Compulsive acts, including those of destruction and greed, also may serve to ward off our fears of death and our sense of anxiety or guilt about our destructive potential and our sense of being less than we might be, although these are often outside of our conscious emotional experience. Even with our reasoning capacity which we idealize and view as limitless, we cannot contain our destructive and possessive urges that manifest themselves as greed and the treating of others, and at times our own selves, as objects. This is carried even to the ends of murder and suicide as a last move by the one who is determined to prove the control, potency, power, and will of the self over and above all else. Therefore, the only way out is to change or transform the self so that the will of the self exclusively for the enhancement of the self is no longer at the center of the self.

Some will set the self aside for the cause of the nation, group, culture, romantic love, or ideology. Eventually the imperfections of even these causes will be seen by observers who are honest with themselves since all such causes are manifestations of merely human life and are attempts at an enlargement of the self by merging with other human selves. Only God can withstand the closest scrutiny over time and remain "ideal." Eventually only God can be seen as worthy of being worshiped. Only God taken into the self at the center can transform a human being, and a self-sacrificing, forgiving God can best compel self-sacrifice and forgiveness.

Even apart from the negative effects of human destructiveness and greed and the losses they will inflict on all of us, the losses we all suffer in life to varying extents make bitterness, cynicism, or despair appear inevitable without a solution offering a larger meaning in this life. A theological solution seems to offer the largest umbrella of meaning and hope by way of becoming loved and accepted (forgiven) as we are and then being loving, accepting, and forgiving toward others. Without this meaning many would have probably become either despondent and despairing or bitter and then destructive.

It appears that it is precisely because of all the pain and suffering in the world and our inability to make adequate sense of it or find any meaning in it that many reject God as a potential reality, let alone as the primary reality. We find it so very difficult to believe in an all-powerful and yet all-loving or good God in the face of the magnitude of the suffering we see around us and in the news daily. In rejecting God because of the presence of so much pain and grief, we reject the very way that offers the best hope of making any meaning of our chaotic world and of that which appears to be evil.

The cause of most of the evil around us is due to the unleashing of our potential to destroy. Our destructive potential is best and most effectively contained in relatedness to God when we hold this God to be one who permits the evil done by others, but love

111

this God anyway. Then any feelings of frustration or rage we have are bound up by feelings of love. Our feelings about loss may be best resolved in the context of this God, as we "forgive" God for what he has allowed to happen and forgive others too.

Numerous things that cause pain and are not due to human design, such as natural disasters and accidents, are not evil *per se* since there was no malevolent intent behind them. Yet they cause great pain and are sad or even tragic and terrible events. There is no evil intent in these events since the God of *agape* love would not *cause* that which is not contained by *agape* love. If God has *caused* the disasters, then they are not evil since they serve some greater good. The really tough question comes then with what God permits to happen. Are all things permitted by God also somehow ultimately good and contained by his *agape* love? Should we take whatever God permits to happen to us as an opportunity for growth toward God and toward somehow working on our spirit or soul? It is possible to try to do this while at the same time working to change that which we sense to be wrong.

But what if the suffering is the result of the evil actions of others? What about the Holocaust? Are events such as this to be used for spiritual growth? Our tendency to identify "the good" and "the bad" makes this terribly difficult and we resist making anything good from that which is so horrible. It would seem to be impossible to put into words what it would be like to contain such rage in God's *agape* love and become forgiving. To become destructive and multiply evil by evil in revenge is our all-too-human inclination and such a large part of our interpersonal, societal, and global turmoil.

Has God ordained it in creation that we will need to reach for him to live this life well? Does some part of us become more perfect through and by the pain we experience which then works to turn us from having the will of the self-centered self at the center of our being? This is the will that craves to be in control of all, have more and more pleasure, and greatly fears loss and pain. Can we believe that this will might be transformed by the experience of God's *agape* love at the center of our being which then functions as the container of our being? Human self-centeredness and grandiosity lead us to reject such a view and its consequences and lead us to refuse to believe that we could be the objects of such a design. Therefore, we are thwarted in our wishes to transcend our pain and suffering caused by our will to be autonomous selves, and our excessive attachment to ourselves as selves. Because of this will of part of the self which resists letting go of itself, only a profound, all-encompassing emotion coupled with thought and intuition in synchrony with that which is beyond us can accomplish change to this degree of transformation. Without the emotional element of the experience, it appears that most people would not change substantially. This is true of most of the accounts of such changes reported by William James in *The Varieties Of Religious Experience.*

In order to resist this change and the feared loss of the self (actually the submission of the self), the will of the self attempts to fortify itself by means of identifying with potent inner forces and basic urges. These include the wish to create or the quest for that which is perfect and the wish to eliminate or control that which is feared. Identification with the former causes, among other things, a search for perfection (something we sense as sacred) and the desire to create or experience it. Therefore, there is eventually an inner push to find something sensed as Holy or Divine. Identification with the latter leads to destructive acts, death, and possible glorification of related pursuits by way of association with people, groups, or ideologies that seem to fortify the sense of potency and power of the will of self alone. In this mode we attempt to avoid being destroyed by that which we fear by becoming that which others will fear. We then become the "badness" or evil we despised so that we might control it. Therefore, in order to contain the powers of destruction within us (our rage and despair as a result of seeing and experiencing the losses inherent in life), and in order not to become part of the destruction, the grounding and containing of the self in *agape* love appears necessary. Arriving at the position to experience *agape* love and the willingness to try to live with *agape* love at the center of our being may require a belief in the being of God and a willingness to interpret experience as if it were in relation to that God.

113

Since life on earth is so full of tragedy and pain for many and no one escapes it entirely, it seems that in order to avoid the conclusion that existence is random and cruel, we must eventually believe that human life is an often tragic but mysteriously precious drama of human beings rejecting self-centeredness and self-absorption in order to find the truest wonderment of the self as a part of that which is transcendent — God. This is "redemption" defined as the recovering of ownership by the paying of a particular sum. Redemption comes about in large part because of and by the way of suffering, and yet, in spite of suffering, since it may become the occasion for forgiveness. If human experience has been created to unfold in this way then God is a God of suffering, who suffers with us, since this God has incorporated suffering into creation. Perhaps the means by which we endure emotional pain is the pivotal point of human experience such that through our enduring whatever comes to us, in *agape* love and forgiveness we may participate in the meaning of this life as God has established it. This needn't mean passive acceptance of injustices done to us. Rather, we can endure best with a response that also affirms our own self as a valuable part of God's creation.

The experience of God offers true transformation by way of the integration of the seemingly horrible with the wonderful, and the mending of that which is evil with that which is perfect. This is a transformation by suffering that we would probably never choose intentionally. Yet when this path is given to us, we must actively live it out well or surrender in despair until the despair itself offers a new opportunity for redemptive suffering and transformation. In this way we each become a bit like God, not by becoming powerful or by being worshiped, but by suffering and loving in spite of suffering that we might weep for all persons as we would have wept for ourselves and as God weeps for all of us. From the tears spring the deepest love, transformation, hope, and rebirth.

Application

The application sections are designed to provide questions to answer, imagery/visualization exercises, passages to mediate on, and tasks to facilitate the goal of being more at one with God. This includes being more like God, more in harmony with the best discernment of the intentions of God, and being all that God would have you be to the fullest of your capacity. The wording used is based on this goal. If you have a different spiritual goal, modify the wordings to fit your situation. Likewise, the wording often uses Jesus (or Christ) as the window to understand the nature and the intentions of God. The goal is not self-development, self-actualization, or the development of one aspect of the self just to have more of some attribute or to be more developed. The goal is to transform the self so that the Spirit of God directing the image of God within is at the center of the self and a oneness with God is fostered. The goal is then to carry out the intentions of God here and now and to offer yourself to the service of that goal.

We have often heard of humans having been viewed as minds trapped in bodies. These tasks propose that we are in a sense souls trapped in personalities. This means simply that our habits, or how we are, often outweigh and get the better of our innermost intentions. Part of our work then is to let some aspects of our personalities, specifically the overly self-centered ones, recede so that the image of God within might come forth more.

To complete the questions it may be best to get in a comfortable seat, let all distractions go, and let your body and mind get very comfortable. To assist in recalling or imagining something, visualizing it as vividly as possible will usually help as will making some notes about your experience.

115

1. Describe a time in your life — just take whatever comes to mind — when you sensed that you were for that moment in time the most at one with God that you have been.

What were you doing?

What were you thinking?

What were you feeling?

How did others around you respond?

What led up to your doing this?

How did it come to be that you did it?

Afterwards how did you feel about it?

Afterwards what did you think about it?

2. Describe another such time, answering all the same questions for it.

3. And another —

4. What similarities between these times can you find?

5. Do you notice differences in how you feel about something versus how you think about it? What might this mean for you?

Sometimes trying to get your "sense" of an experience brings thought and feeling together more.

6. Describe a time in your life — again take whatever comes up — when you felt closest to God. Answer all the follow-up questions in number 1 for this and generate three or so more times as with number 1.

7. Do experiences of closeness and oneness match for you?

8. Repeat question 1 but focus on a time you sensed you were for that moment being at one with the Spirit of Jesus or being Christ-like. Respond to all the follow-up questions in question 1 for this too. Explore several of these times.

9. Now focus on a time when you were most fully being all or the very best you can imagine God would have you be. Complete the follow-up questions to question 1 with this episode and with several other episodes like it.

10. If you were to be all that God would have you be, what do you imagine would be different? Describe the details a video camera would show.

11. When does it usually occur for you to feel more of a oneness with God? With others? Are there any times when it usually or always happens? Are there any times when it never happens?

12. Where does this sense of oneness with God usually occur?

13. Where is it more likely to occur?

Where does it always occur?

Where does it never occur?

Give general and specific locations.

14. Where does the sense of being more Christ-like occur? Repeat the questions under number 13 for this.

15. Where does it occur that you sense you are being the very best God intends you to be? Repeat the questions under number 13 here too.

16. What does being at one with God look like for you if we were to observe it?

17. What would a videotape of the action show?

18. What would being more like Jesus or more a part of Christ look like and what would a videotape show?

19. What would being the very most God would have you be look like and show on a videotape?

20. What would we see happening in terms of postures, gestures, sequences of action, interaction, and talk in number 15, number 16, number 17, and number 18?

21. With whom does it occur that you are being more at one with God and what do others do or say before, during, and after you do this?

22. With whom does it occur that you are being more Christ-like and what do others do or say before, during, and after you do this?

23. With whom does it occur that you are being the most (or best) God would have you be and what do others do or say before, during, and after you do this?

24. Look over your responses to all of the questions and notice the exceptions to your observations when the usual rules do not seem to apply.

25. What becomes possible because of your being more at one with God?

26. What might others see you do that is related to being more at one with God?

27. What are your explanations as to how you come to this way of being?

28. How will you know when you are being at one with God more continuously?

29. Thinking of Jesus as the vine and us as the branches, it is also fitting to think of a oneness with Jesus or being a part of Jesus or the Spirit of Jesus. Repeat any of the items you wish to that referred to a oneness with God using instead a oneness with Jesus, a oneness with Christ, a part of Jesus, or a part of Christ.

Imagery/Visualization Exercise

If you were to wake up from sleep and notice that you were now being much more at one with God (or a branch of the vine of Christ), what would you first notice as different?

What would others notice?

What do you imagine would have had to occur while you slept for you to be this way?

When have you been like this — even for a moment — before?

What are some other times you've been like this?

What enabled you to be this way?

What did you do that helped?

If you have described the differences as things you will not do then what will you be doing instead? Describe specific actions.

What will others notice is different about you?

How will you feel about others noticing this?

Experience some of that feeling right now for a while and describe it.

What else will others notice?

What specific small steps toward being more at one with God might you begin now? What would that accomplishment look like on a video?

What else might you do toward this goal that is a small but specific step? And what else?

Are you ready, without feeling pushed or rushed, to do two of those things next week? Only do so if you're really ready.

What obstacles might get in the way of following through on your plans?

What can you do, specifically, in response to each obstacle?

What resources are there (inner and outer) for you to engage for help to manage the obstacles?

Inventory

What is your deepest desire? If you could have anything or situation, what would it be?

What else?

And what else?

What is your strongest wish?

What else?

And what else?

What would be the consequences, really, if this desire came to be fulfilled? Answer this for each desire and each wish.

Would there be some "cost" or negative consequences if this desire came to be fulfilled? Consider this for each desire and every wish that you identified as significant for you.

What is your most intense fear?

What else?

And what else?

What is your most frequent fear?

What else?

And what else?

What is your longest lasting but current fear?

What else?

And what else?

What do your most vague anxieties seem to be about?

What else?

And perhaps what else?

What are your worst, most nagging doubts about?

List three, four, or more in addition.

What is your most intense inner conflict?

What is your most frequent inner conflict?

What is your most lasting but current conflict?

List your most intense, frequent, lasting external conflicts too. For each fear, anxiety, doubt, or inner and external conflict, what would be different in your life if it were resolved or put to the side?

How (for each) would your day-to-day life be different if it were gone or receded to the background of your awareness?

Would there be any costs or less-than-pleasant consequences if these changes were to occur?
    For each desire, fear, doubt, or conflict, list what its existence prevents for you.

If something is prevented by the presence of desire, fear, doubt, or conflict, specify what actions you will do instead.

Identify a fear that you have overcome or, if not completely over-come, in part.

What enabled you to do this?

What did you do that contributed to this process?

Identify two or three more fears that you have overcome at any time in your life and note what led you to this for each. Also, note what you did that contributed to the positive outcome.

Do the same as you have done for several fears with doubts, inner and outer conflicts, and desires that you feel have been excessive.

Noting these successes you have had and your own contribution to them, do you wish to make some changes with your current desires, fears, doubts, and conflicts?

If so, what?

What specific small things can you do this week to begin to let go of or let recede into the background a fear, doubt, conflict, or excessive desire?

What will you be doing instead?

How will the difference look on a video?

The questions in this Application section are substantially influenced by the work of Cade and O'Hanlon, DeJong and Berg, O'Hanlan and Beadle, and Oliver, Hasz and Richburg.

References And Bibliography

Augustine (1986). *Confessions* (R.S. Pine-Coffin, Trans.). New York: Dorset Press. (Original work published 357.)

Becker, E. (1973). *The Denial Of Death*. New York: The Free Press.

Cade, B. and O'Hanlon, W. (1993). *A Brief Guide To Brief Therapy*. New York: W.W. Norton and Co.

Cashdèn, S. (1988). *Object Relations Therapy: Using The Relationship*. New York: W.W. Norton.

Constantine, L. L. (1986). *Family Paradigms: The Practice Of Theory In Family Therapy*. New York: Guilford Press.

DeJong, P. and Berg, I. K. (1998). *Learners Workbook For Interviewing For Solutions*. New York: Brooks/Cole Publishing Co.

Freud, S. (1964). *The Future Of An Illusion*. (Revised Anchor Books Edition) J. P. Streachey (Ed.) and W.D. Robson-Scott (Trans.). Garden City, New York: Doubleday. (Original work published 1928.)

Freud, S. (1968). Transference. In J. Riviere (Ed.), *A General Introduction To Psychoanalysis* (pp. 438-455). New York: Washington Square Press. (Original work published 1924.)

Heimann, P. (1952). Notes on the theory of the life and death instincts. In J. Riviere (Ed.), *Developments In Psychoanalysis*. (pp. 321-337). London: Hogarth Press.

James, W. (1902). *The Varieties Of Religious Experience*. Toronto: Random House.

Kernberg, O. (1985). *Borderline Conditions And Pathological Narcissism*. Northvale, New Jersey: Jason Aronson, Inc.

Kierkegaard, S. (1944). Either/Or A Fragment Of Life. (Vols. 1 & 2.) D. F. Swenson and L. M. Swenson (Trans.). London: Oxford University Press.

Kierkegaard, S. (1955). *The Gospel Of Our Sufferings*. A.S. Aldsworth and W. S. Ferrie (Trans.). Grand Rapids, Michigan: William B. Eerdmans Publishing Company.

Klein, M. (1952). Some theoretical conclusions regarding the emotional life of the infant. In J. Riviere (Ed.), *Developments In Psychoanalysis*. (pp. 198-270). London: Hogarth Press.

Kushner, H. (1981). *When Bad Things Happen To Good People*. New York: Avon Books.

Mahler, M., Pine, F., and Bergman, A. (1975). *The Psychological Birth Of The Human Infant*. New York: Basic Books.

May, H. and Metzger, B. (Eds.). (1965). *The Oxford Annotated Bible With Apocrypha* (Revised Standard Version). New York: Oxford University Press.

Miller, N. (1948). Theory and experiment relating psychoanalytic displacement to stimulus-response generalization. *Journal Of Abnormal And Social Psychology*, pp. 43, 155-178.

O'Hanlon, W. and Beadle, S. (1997). *A Guide To Possibility Land*. New York: W.W. Norton and Co.

Oliver, G., Hasz, M. and Richburg, M. (1997). *Promoting Change Through Brief Therapy In Christian Counseling*. Wheaton, Illinois: Tyndale House.

Tillich, P. (1952). *The Courage To Be*. New Haven: Yale University Press.

Vanauken, S. (1977). *A Severe Mercy*. New York: HarperCollins.

World Bible Publishers, Inc. (1989). *King James Version Of The Bible*. Iowa Falls, Iowa.